Sixty-Six Years
a Cycle Tourist

Sixty-Six Years

a Cycle Tourist

CLIFF PRATT

The Pentland Press
Edinburgh – Cambridge – Durham

© Cliff Pratt, 1994

First published in 1994
by The Pentland Press Ltd
1 Hutton Close
South Church
Bishop Auckland
Durham

British Library
Cataloguing in Publication Data

A Catalogue record for this book
is available from the British Library

ISBN 1–85821–229-4

Typeset by Carnegie Publishing Ltd., 18 Maynard St., Preston
Printed and bound by Antony Rowe Ltd., Chippenham

To my dear wife Ida,
for her help, encouragement
and companionship
in many of my activities.

Contents

Acknowledgements

First and foremost I must thank my nephew David for his considerable help with this project and without whose encouragement it would never have seen the light of day. I would also like to thank my old cycling colleagues who have reminded me of happenings in the distant past; the Cyclists' Touring Club, for permission to use various references from Bill Oakley's book *Winged Wheel*; D. A. Moore and the Temple Press for use of certain York Rally photographs; and also my brother Norman, for the sketches.

Abbreviations

AIT	Alliance Internationale de Tourisme
CTC	Cyclists' Touring Club
DA	District Association

Foreword

IT IS A TRUISM that you don't have to scratch a dedicated cyclist very deep to reveal not only a fund of anecdotes but also a range of experience and diversity of interest often astonishing to those unacquainted with what might otherwise be thought a simple and very basic pastime. When, as for the author of this book, the dedication and experience have spanned some seventy years, it needs but little imagination to realise at the outset that here is a life story with a difference. It is a tale of travelling through much of the twentieth century on two wheels; it is a social history, it is an enthusiast's expression of the joys and rewards brought to him in his long association with the cycling game, all rolled into one.

Cliff Pratt has not simply ridden a bicycle all his life; he has lived cycling. Wide-ranging tourist, both at home and abroad; cycle-shop owner and bike builder; clubman; national administrator and organiser; wise counsellor and valued friend; he has seen so much and enjoyed it all – uphill and down. His has been an observant eye, too, capturing the miles and the memories with a photographic skill to delight his contemporaries and to illustrate this story he has to tell.

If you read this book as a fellow cyclist, you will find many a mirror image of your own delight in the way you have chosen to travel and explore, coupled of course with the many facets of the author's own experiences, enthusiasms and involvement with all things cycling. For those less familiar with the world of the silent wheel and the attractions of cycling club life, there will be much to discover and admire – perhaps even to astonish and amaze. Whatever your persuasions or inclinations, however, read it as Cliff Pratt has lived it, simply for the pleasure and sheer variety of it all.

Les Warner MBE

For many years Les Warner was one of the principal administrators of international cycle touring. A life-long cyclist (as is his wife Sheila), he was the National Secretary of the Cyclists' Touring Club from 1959 to 1980. A past president of the CTC, winner of the Sir Alfred Bird Memorial Prize in 1967, he was also president of the Cycle Touring Commission of the Alliance Internationale de Tourisme. He is currently a Honorary Vice-President of the CTC.

Les Warner.

How it all started

ALTHOUGH I was always keen on most outdoor activities I was nineteen before my interest in cycling was triggered off in 1927, although I have to thank my younger brother Noel for inducing me to buy a bicycle.

My only claim to a cycling background was that I understood that my mother and father were members of the Victoria cycling club back in the 1890s. My father, a studio photographer, set up in business on his own in 1906 and it was here, while still of tender tears, that I can recall seeing my father's cycle, then pensioned off, rusting its life away in an outhouse.

Unfortunately, in my ignorance, the cycle I acquired (with the financial assistance of one of my colleagues in the timber merchant's office in which I worked), was a full-blown roadster, complete with 28"× 1½" wheels, roller lever (rod) brakes, and a freewheel providing a single gear of 75". Thus equipped, my career took off with a ride to Brantingham Dale, although this modest start quickly led to more ambitious rides, while in the October I realised my ambition to 'see the moors'.

Of course, by this time, I had realised that I had the wrong type of cycle so I 'swapped' it for what was then known as a 'lightweight racer'. Now this was equipped with 26" × 1¼" wheels, caliper brakes and a rear wheel fitted with a double-sided hub providing a fixed sprocket 75" gear on one side and a 63" freewheel on the other. The caliper brakes were interesting; they were of French construction and the finish was of black paint – even the cables, as there were no plastic covered cables then. An unfortunate consequence of this finish was that after a while they became rather rusty.

Incidentally, chromium plating hadn't come on the scene at this time and the usual 'bright' parts – rims, handlebars, chainwheel and cranks etc. were nickel plated which unfortunately soon became dull and had to be polished. Actually the Hercules Company were experimenting with chromium plating but the results were very unsatisfactory. When chromium plating finally arrived it certainly brightened up even the cheapest cycle. On the more expensive clubman's cycle the chromium was applied over a base of copper and nickel and was very durable.

Having become the proud possessor of a 'real' cycle I was fortunate enough to meet Bob Threadfall who introduced me to the Cyclists'

Touring Club — surely the wisest move I could have made. My first ride with CTC was on 1 April 1928 when I joined the Hardriders run to Hackness and that run might easily have been my one and only run with the club, as I received a decidedly odd reception. Arriving at the starting place at the corner of Inglemire Lane, I was at first completely ignored by the collection of 'old hands'. One of them finally came over and, after studying my newly acquired BLUE cycle for some time, and without a word of greeting, said, 'Couldn't you have got a black 'un?' I then became aware of the fact that all the other cycles were black. This really knocked the stuffing out of me but happily another one of the members approached and made me feel more at ease. This was Harry Wharton, the leader of the Hardriders, who later did such marvellous work for the club by editing the District Association Magazine *Herda*, and writing a weekly account of our runs which was printed in the *Sports Mail*. During the war he kept in touch with most of our members; then in the forces, by means of a newsletter.

Later I became better acquainted with George Reeder, who was my first contact, and we even toured together in Norway, but George was most definitely a 'one off' and could come out with the most remarkable comments. On one occasion, on learning that I had been cycling on the Saturday afternoon (we worked Saturday mornings in those days) he said, 'Don't you get enough cycling on Sunday?' But George was responsible for what must be the perfect retort. Meeting a youngster with bike trouble, as was our practice, we stopped to offer assistance, at which point George took out and unrolled his, to us, familiar tool kit. Now George's tool kit was a sight for sore eyes, containing, as it did, every imaginable tool and spare. Well, on seeing George's amazing tool kit, the youngster's eyes simply goggled, and he remarked, 'What do you carry all that lot around with you for?', to which George replied, 'For silly buggers like you.'

I really don't remember much about the first ride with the club, though one incident does stick in my memory. Arriving at Driffield Market Place on the outward run I was astonished when the entire club dismounted and commenced removing their rear wheels which were reversed and refitted. The reason for this astonishing behaviour became apparent. Having ridden the twenty flat miles from home on the large fixed gears, the lower freewheel was brought into use for the ensuing hilly miles over the Wolds. This was normal practice apparently!

With this ride, I became firmly established as a member of the Hull and East Riding District Association of the Cyclists' Touring Club, an association which has existed to this day!

Road Conditions

When I first started cycling, the Wolds roads were in a diabolical state. Running out in a northerly or north-westerly direction they were quite reasonable as far as say Wetwang or Driffield, but beyond that you were more or less on the foundations. In the summer time (the dry season – sometimes), one came upon long stretches of road which consisted of loose stones, and inches of white chalk dust which soon coated one's clothing, while in the winter – now, that was the most memorable. The chalk dust had now become something in the nature of white paint which played the dickens with bearings, chain and clothing. These conditions were accepted as inevitable so we just 'ploughed on' regardless.

One of our members was a bit of a wizard on the mouth-organ which he insisted on playing on every available occasion. Who'll forget the memorable day when he rode up Fimber Hill – ruts and all – still playing his mouth-organ! Of course when the Wolds roads were tarred a few years later, it came as a great relief. 'Pop' Pudsey (he was a bit older than us) told us that he could remember when the road down Arras hill into Market Weighton was well rutted just as the Wolds roads were.

The DA Insurance Scheme

In the thirties, there was a dreadful lot of unemployment – far worse than today – and many members were affected. Even those working often only received £2.00 per week, and I remember the man who drove the Railway Parcels van which called at the shop telling us that his weekly wage was 30 shillings (£1.50).

Perhaps it was this state of affairs that led to the establishment of the DA insurance scheme in 1928, following a suggestion by Harry Suddaby. The idea was to provide some insurance cover in the case of accidental damage sustained on club runs. The annual premium was set at 1d. per year.

Growing Enthusiasm

In those days my enthusiasm for cycling developed by the day. Every opportunity was taken to be out on the road, while weekends were looked forward to with barely suppressed anticipation. I have been told that I was always so anxious that as little cycling time as possible was lost that I used to take my meals with my watch propped up in front of me.

Noel was often my companion and I can recall one particular ride that April that included beautiful Rosedale and those magnificent views across the moors. Then on 6 May 1928 I enjoyed my first all night ride, this time with the Hardriders. Leaving Hull at about midnight we delved far into the West Riding, with Upper Nidderdale and the newly constructed Scar House Reservoir our target. Then it was up and over the top of Dead Man's Hill into Coverdale. This was the first of numerous all night rides. On 8 July I joined the club for a 220-mile run for the club's 24-hour certificate, but I did many all night rides alone – there was something magical about cycling at night. The silence and almost complete absence of motor traffic was a joy in itself, whilst often a barn owl would accompany you as you rode along, flying parallel over the hedge tops. Strange how simple things will often bring great pleasure and linger in the memory. While on our way to Derbyshire at Whitsuntide in 1930, we were descending a steep hill with the moonlight flashing in and out among the trees, when we became aware of the most glorious scent of hawthorn which was enhanced by the cool night air.

So often I have found that an ordinary ride can be turned into something special by a single incident. On one occasion it was our luck to see a family of stoats, with the mother dashing frantically up and down the hedgerow whilst the youngsters selected tufts of grass to hide behind, just as we had seen baby plovers do up on the moors. The action of the parents was, of course, to distract attention, just as was the feigned injury of the adult plovers. Then on one occasion it was a pair of 'boxing hares' and then there was the sighting of a little owl.

It wasn't so long ago that I witnessed a sight that will remain in my memory for many a day. Leaving Broomfleet on the Humber, we made our way to Weighton Lock, then, turning northward on the footpath alongside the Market Weighton Canal, we were greeted by the sight of a family of swans cruising majestically towards us. One parent bird led the way followed by six cygnets with the other parent bringing up the rear. A delightful picture, but, inevitably the camera was at home!

Then a memory of a different sort. It was on a Thursday afternoon section run, way back in the thirties when, having had tea at Holme on Spalding Moor, we were enjoying the ride home in the crisp air of a November evening. Our attention was drawn to strange lights in the sky. Dismounting, we were entertained by a wonderful display of the aurora borealis (Northern Lights). So far as I was concerned this was a once in a lifetime experience.

Checking my diaries I see that I accumulated 12,313 miles that first year but this total grew in subsequent years to reach 18,165 in 1930. But

I must stress that pure mileage was never the aim – it was just the sheer joy of cycling. At the same time however we were very keen on moorland crossings which, as often as not, were included in our day's itinerary. Wheeldale Moor (before the Lyke Wake business cropped up), Blakey Topping, Lilla Cross and the Bridestones come readily to mind.

Just a Cycle Tourist

Jack Kirk had competed in the Olympic Games as a cyclist in 1910 and later entered the cycle trade, firstly, I believe, in Brook Street, but later with a fine shop in Newland Avenue. He was a member of the Hull Thursday Road Club and did much useful work assisting the members in their racing activities. I used to go to Jack for all my cycling requirements and it was there that I met some of the leading lights in the HTRC, and thought what a decent lot they were, though I had been led to believe that racing men were rather 'beyond the pale'. Incidentally, I understood that the racing man's opinion of the CTC was that they were a lot of snobs! How laughable – but all that nonsense changed in subsequent years. Jack seemed to take an interest in my exploits, especially long distance rides, and did his best to persuade me to take up this form of racing. But I wasn't to be tempted, realising full well that racing would have a dire effect on my first love – cycle touring. In any case I have always regarded myself as a non-competitive sort.

The Derailleur Gear

It all seemed to be happening around this period and 29 November 1929 must be regarded as a red letter day for that was the day I had my first derailleur gear fitted, revolutionising my activities. Of course variable gears were not entirely new – the Sturmey Archer hub gear had existed for some time – but the club fraternity had decided that the Sturmey was not acceptable! It is true that there was some definite loss of power with the hub gear and a peculiar 'soft' feel to one's pedalling; anyhow it was taboo and no self-respecting clubman dared turn up on a run with a Sturmey. But a very good friend of cycling, Louis Camillis, brought over from France the first derailleur gear to be introduced to British cyclists. It was a three-speed gear using a standard ½" × ⅛" chain which, with various sprocket sizes available, made a wide variation of gears possible. This was not so with the Sturmey which, although a three-speed, only offered a fixed ratio for upper and lower gears. I think I must have been one of the first British cyclists to benefit from this introduction but soon they were being fitted by club cyclists, particularly the tourists, throughout the land. Soon after the arrival of the Cyclo Derailleur other variable gears came along, the most popular being the TriVelox, a British made gear that by its construction obviated the chain being out of line on the outer sprockets, although it was soon found that rapid wear of the hub spines was a serious problem. It was fitted to many mass-produced tandems which sold in vast quantities in the thirties.

The Weaver's Wagger

Now Albert Weaver was one of the most fastidious chaps in the club – we used to call him 'the immaculate Albert'. Well, like many of us, he used to object to being sprayed with mud and water by the rider in front of him. But Albert did something about it – he designed the Weaver's Wagger and submitted it to Bluemells who considered it a good idea and produced one which, after receiving Albert's approval, they marketed. What it amounted to was a rear mudguard extension, which reached almost down to the road and terminated with a mud flap. It was also supplied with an extra set of stays for stability. The Weavers Wagger was a huge success and it became an unwritten law that if you rode with the club you must fit one. What became of it?

Travel Talks

In the twenties and particularly in the thirties, the Travel Talk (or Lantern Lecture) became very popular, the principle lecturers being W. M. Robinson (Warfarer), Fitzwater Wray (Kuklos) and Nevill Whall (Hodites), who gave their talks, illustrated by lantern slides, throughout the country. One of my earliest runs was when, in the company of Trav Hunter, we rode up to Stockton-on-Tees to hear Kuklos, returning next day with Harry Wharton and Bob Craggy by way of Rudland Rigg. I attended what must have been one of Hodites' last talks in Bradford in 1939, and had the honour of moving a 'vote of thanks', whilst I gave my Yugoslavia talk in the same hall a month later.

Norway was the chosen touring ground for a party of Hull members in 1932 and afterwards a travel talk based on the tour and illustrated by lantern slides proved to be the first of a series during the thirties. At the time I wrote an article regarding Norway as a cycle touring country and this appeared in the *Gazette* (or *Cycle Touring* as they call it in these days). This led to me receiving numerous enquiries for information and seemed to start a great popularity for Norway with CTC members.

Following the success of the Norwegian expedition, similar tours were carried out in the great mountain regions of Europe, such as the Austrian, Swiss, French, Italian and Bavarian Alps and the fantastic Dolomites, with Yugoslavia the last of the series.

After each tour I prepared a travel talk illustrated by lantern slides and I must say that the production of these was a very involved business which took ages before the $3\frac{1}{4}'' \times 3\frac{1}{4}''$ slide was achieved. How different today when the $2'' \times 2''$ transparency, in its cardboard mount, can be immediately projected. Apart from the initial showing in Hull I also gave shows in Bradford, Cardiff, Darlington, Grimsby, Huddersfield, Leeds, Liverpool, Manchester, Mansfield, Newcastle-on-Tyne, Nottingham, Sheffield etc. For the Yugoslavia show in Hull we had an attendance of 650 in the old Royal Institution, thanks to an enthusiastic ticket-selling campaign by our members. Incidentally the Royal Institution, the then principal lecture hall, was demolished during one of Hull's many blitzes. These out of town shows involved much travelling and I recall the occasion when I combined a short cycle tour with a mini-lecture-trip giving shows on successive nights in Sheffield, Mansfield and Nottingham. I certainly knew about it lugging those 30 lbs. of slides up those Derbyshire hills.

I was fortunate in having the assistance of my brother Norman, who provided cartoons depicting humorous incidents which occurred on the tours. These I photographed and converted into slides. Norman was a first class artist and cartoonist, although cartoons were not his principal activity. He worked for the Gaumont British Picture Corporation and used to turn out displays for the promotion of the big pictures as they appeared. Of course my father was an artist so that probably explains a lot! Actually, all my three brothers were skilled in one way or another – all but me; all I could do was ride a bike!

Mainly District Association Affairs

After 1930 my cycling became somewhat restricted for a while, apart from weekends, as the firm got the strange idea that I would make a salesman. I had done some travelling on a fairly local basis for some time but now I was to include such dreadful places as Bradford, Huddersfield, Leeds and Sheffield. I hated it! But all that changed in 1934 when, at last, the opportunity came along and Frank Suddaby and I started our own cycle business.

The shop at 84 Spring Bank had initially only occupied the front of the premises on the ground floor – the sales shop with the workshop behind and all very restricting. But soon we were able to acquire the entire building, thus enabling us to spread our wings somewhat.

At first we didn't need the upper portion of the building and as the club had been considered establishing their own permanent headquarters for some time, the first floor was offered and accepted. The Hull and East Riding District Association of the Cyclists' Touring Club now had its own permanent home and a very handsome sign board was built by two of our joiner members and suitably positioned over the shop. Separate access was provided at the side of the shop.

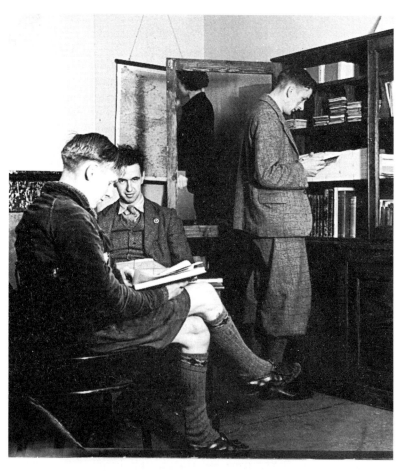

The Hull District Association headquarters.
Left to right: Wilf Rippon, Frank Norgate and Noel Baker.

Open several nights each week in charge of members of the committee (on rota) the headquarters proved very popular. The provision of the library, darts and table tennis were much appreciated facilities as was the darkroom where members could process their own photographs.

But apart from the headquarters, the winter clubroom was held in the Waltham Street schoolroom where Fred Ingilby held sway and provided a first-class programme which ranged from slide shows (the principal entertainment) to concerts, an auction sale, table tennis and photographic competitions. One year, Fred, in an effort to introduce variety into the weekly clubroom activities, invited members to make themselves responsible for a particular evening. This produced some surprising entertainment. Bert 'Tubby' Howell, a wrestling and weight-lifting fanatic, put on a demonstration of these arts, while members were invited to participate. Bert, it should be mentioned, was quite well known in the wrestling world and was once top of the bill at a show in one of the local theatres, being styled 'The Champion of Canada'. Perhaps even more likely to remain in the memory was the night 'Skid' Colman arranged to bring a complete brass band. The noise, that night, was unbelievable – the rafters positively throbbed while members wishing to converse with their neighbour had literally to scream into one another's ears.

In the summer the clubroom moved out into the country to either the Wilson Memorial Hut at Anlaby or the Village Hall in Skidby. Now, who was involved in all these activities? Names which come readily to mind are Parker-Walker (President); A. F. (Gill) Gilleard (Treasurer) and his wife Marie (an early Social Secretary), Bob Craggy, Harry Wharton, George Reeder, Eddie Rayner, Tom Webster, Ken Hughes (Hardriders Section), Les Theadgold (Intermediates Section), Harry Dale (General Section), George Coates (Social Section) and Eric Sanderson (Scarborough Section).

Then there was Gill Dosser, Hon. Secretary of the Hull and East Riding Road Club, our racing offshoot, with membership restricted to members of the CTC. But we had other sections for such specialists as Photographers, Campers and the Thursday Afternoon Section.

Many of our members belonged to the Youth Hostels Association and would often participate in Hostel weekends – riding out to some hostel in North Yorkshire or the Dales on the Saturday and returning home on the Sunday.

Fred Greenway is perhaps, best remembered for his incredible feat when, after an unfortunate mishap (not a collision) he rode home from Etton with A BROKEN LEG before receiving attention!

Bernard Outhwaite, another Hardrider who had taken part in our continental tours, did yeoman service for the DA as Hon. Treasurer for a number of years.

Freddy Mackrill was a notable character in cycling circles in the twenties and thirties and his anecdotes dated back to the days of the penny-farthing ('ordinary') races, which were held on the old Boulevard track. Freddy was a painter and decorator by trade and was an unmistakeable figure owing to an unfortunate deformity which gave him a 'hunched' back. He made no pretence of being able to read a map, whilst he had little sense of direction, which was the probable reason why he always endeavoured to ride in company, when his never-ending narratives were greatly enjoyed. Who cared if, sometimes, he strayed into the realms of fantasy? Although then only in his mid-forties we, with whom he often rode, tended to regard him as a likeable old 'has-been'. He was very proud of his Rover cycle, one of the last of a highly respected breed – although his mount bore little resemblance to the original of 1885. The introduction of the Rover, the first 'safety' cycle, really sounded the death knell of the 'ordinary' with its enormous front wheel on which any pretence of gearing was dependent. With the two moderate sized wheels of the Rover, gearing was provided, as now, by a front chainwheel and rear sprocket – with connecting chain!

Wooden rims and handlebars were Freddie's lesser eccentricities, but I liked best his 'pictorial home trainer'. Now Freddie's trainer (home made, of course) in its original form proved too boring – failing to provide him with a realistic enough impression of cycle touring – so he organised a scenic panorama device, coupled to the transmission, to provide a moving picture of the scenery.

Unfortunately, another of Freddie's problems was very poor eyesight, but another of his oddities was that he didn't believe in opticians, whilst glasses he regarded as 'eye crutches'. Hence he must have had a very dim view of things.

Another character of the same period was 'Roma' – I never knew his surname but he was reputed to write cycling notes for a local newspaper under this pen-name. I have no recollection of his ever riding a cycle, but I do know that he ran some sort of cycle repair business with premises somewhere in a passage off Park Street where he entertained the club lads.

A cabinet maker by trade, Norman Woodhead was already a prominent member of the DA when I came on the scene and my memory of him was that on changing his employment, he loaded all his by no means lightweight tools, onto his cycle and pedalled off to meet his new employer at Kilburn. This was Robert Thompson whose well known trademark, the mouse, is to be found in many Yorkshire Churches.

Apart from those already mentioned, others who have been prominent in the DA are many, but those which come to mind are: John Andrews, Doug and Hilda Barker, Alf and Freda Collinson, Freddie Crooks, Lew and Freda Hampshire, Ken Howard, Harry and Freda Johnson, Alf and Doris King, Ernie and Beryl Maynard, Charlie and Lillian Nicholson, Frank and Freda Norgate, Harry Rickles, Wilf Rippon, Henry Spiers and Alf and Ken Starkey.

But we mustn't forget George Munson. I first knew George as a member of the Hardriders in the early thirties, when his enthusiasm and humour seemed to rub off on all he met. During the war and the years following the war, he organised a cycling club at the Ainthorpe Grove School where he was a teacher. This remarkable club, composed mainly of older pupils, was developed very much on the lines of the Hardriders Section and carried out some quite prodigious runs such as Falling Foss, Bransdale and Scugdale, to say nothing of extensive tours of the British Isles and the Alps. Very often, George would be riding tandem with Rita, his wife. George is also a first class photographer and a member of the Hull Photographic Society, whilst he has given many hours of entertainment with his slides and narratives based on his cycling activities.

Mentioning the Anlaby Clubroom reminds me of a most alarming experience way back in the thirties. With brother Noel, we were approaching Anlaby when we were embroiled in a violent thunderstorm, with torrents of rain causing us to 'cape-up'. Continuing, we had not travelled far, however, when a vivid streak of lightning streaked down into a field on our left, followed almost immediately by another which struck the road directly in front of our front wheels. As the lightning struck, several 'roots' broke away, slapping down on the road with a loud hissing sound. Simultaneously, we were both almost blinded by the flash, but when we had recovered, we were relieved to find that we were none the worse!

The East Riding used to be blessed with several toll bridges. The usual toll for cyclists was ½d., although if this could be avoided, so much the better! I remember that on one occasion, during an all night ride, we had occasion to use a toll bridge which then existed at Bubwith. As we approached the bridge in the dead of night we were all sworn to silence, on the pain of death, lest we wake the toll-keeper!

Whilst dealing with this part of the world, I am reminded of the occasion involving the level crossing near Cliffe, three miles east of Selby. Now there was a regular pea-soup fog at the time and the railway line crossed the road at an acute angle. Well, as Eddie Rayner and I approached the crossing, we were astounded to come across Reg (Skid) Colman, stationary, evidently waiting for the gates to open for road traffic to proceed. The snag was that he was actually facing up the line having become completely disorientated.

I Become DA Secretary

When I joined the club in 1927 the District Association Secretary was Bob Craggy who had taken over from Eddie Bacon seven years previously. However, by 1934 Bob made it known that he thought he had been in the job long enough – he had been an excellent Secretary and many were sorry to see him relinquish the position – and in a moment of weakness I agreed to stand for the job, though afterwards I had severe doubts as I didn't think I could live up to Bob's standard! Anyhow I was elected – if that's the right word (actually no-one else allowed their name to go forward) – but it soon looked as though I had chosen the entirely wrong time to take on the job.

It seemed that at a General Meeting held in London it had been decided that public meetings be organised by the District Associations at Birmingham, Bristol, Liverpool, Manchester and Hull (among other places). The purpose of these meetings was to condemn (a) the approval of cycle path construction, and (b) the scandalous conduct of coroners' courts when considering fatal road accidents.

Well, our committee readily decided that we should play our part and the suggestion was made that we should book the Waltham Street school-room (our normal meeting place). I felt that if we were to gain the interest of the press and public we should be bold and book the City Hall. After much scoffing and remarks such as 'you'll look a right idiot if only a handful turn up', I got my way and we packed the City Hall! Incidentally this was the occasion when brother Noel nearly set the City Hall on fire while taking a flash-light photograph with a shovel full of flash powder!

The following year (1935) being the twenty-fifth anniversary of the accession to the throne of the club's patron, HM King George V, a great relay ride was held. A route of 2,250 miles in fifteen days involved teams of riders from forty-two District Associations carrying a message of congratulation and good wishes. This was illuminated on vellum and was eventually signed by every Lord Mayor in England and Wales (Lord Provost in Scotland). Needless to say I was responsible for the Hull DA's part in the event. Our party took over from the North Lincs group at the Corporation Pier and took it to the Lord Mayor of York when the Mid-Yorks DA took over.

Kiplingcotes rally (1930). The tube burst at 4,800 pumpfuls!

Round Britain relay ride (1934). C.P. hands a message of greeting for H.M.
King George V to the Lord Mayor of York for signature.

Since its formation way back in 1925 the activities of the DA were conducted in a pretty business-like manner as, for instance, the establishment of a destination plate at our meeting place at the corner of Inglemire Lane. This plate was of bronze and had been approved by the City Engineer. On the day the run took place a specially prepared gummed label would be attached to the plate by the run's leader. This bore particulars as to the section, time of departure, destination and route to be followed. This was for the benefit of late-comers! Another action was the despatch, in advance, of a specially produced postcard to the proprietor of the chosen tea-place, advising our likely time of arrival, numbers, etc. Incidentally he was also expected to provide suitable accommodation for our cycles – and washing facilities! Those were the days. Imagine what the response would be today.

In one of our pre-war DA handbooks are listed sixty-five appointments used by our members. These were mostly in East Yorkshire although many were in the Dales. Perhaps the most popular were Bishop Wilton (The Fleece), Driffield (Harpers Picture House Café), Goman Castle Farm (Bugthorpe) (Mrs Gofton), Kirby Moorside (The George and Dragon), Lund (Wellington Inn), Middleton-on-the-Wolds (Mrs Crompton), Muker (Mrs Kilburn – Swale Farm), Thornton Dale (Mrs Maidment), West Witton (Mrs Cottingham), and Wold Newton (The Anvil Arms). Incidentally, Mrs Crompton's establishment at Middleton-on-the-Wolds still retains its connection with cycling and the club as this is now the home of my nephew, David Pratt, who apart from having numerous friends in the club, has also, almost from its inception, been Hon. Treasurer, transport manager, mechanic and what have you of the Beech Holme Tandem Club (for blind back riders).

To give an indication of how prices have changed since those pre-war days, it is interesting to know that the usual charge for tea, (provided with your own food), would be 6d. (2½p), for as much as you could drink, and – in the colder weather – a roaring fire provided. A full tea (say meat, eggs, fruit and bread and butter) would costs 1s. 6d. (7½p). Overnight accommodation as listed in the CTC Handbook would be 4s. 0d. (20p) for bed and breakfast (sometimes even less!).

It was in 1936 that the DA was instrumental in having one of the club's special 'STEEP HILL' signs established on Leavening hill, with the co-operation of the East Riding Council. Incidentally it was on Leavening hill, in 1932, that I was involved in both of my only tumbles from my cycle – normally I stayed in the saddle! What happened? Well, we always looked forward to the long swooping descent of Leavening and I quickly attained a fair old speed as I approached the awkward corner which swung away to the left. Seeing a gap on the inside I yelled to George Munson, who was ahead of me 'Coming through on your inside.' Unfortunately, he failed to hear me, and decided, at that very moment, to cut in to the nearside. I had two alternatives – either slap straight into him, or let go of the brakes and hurtle through before he closed the gap completely! I made it but by then was travelling at such a rate that I failed to get around the corner. That taught me a lesson, but at the time my one thought was, would whatever I had done to my arm affect our Norwegian tour due shortly afterwards? Then on the second occasion Ken and I were descending the hill on our newly acquired tandem at what I considered at the time to be a heck of a speed when, arriving at the bottom, we failed to negotiate the water splash, which used to exist at that point and, well, we came a right old purler! Now, as I was on the rear seat at the time I disclaimed all responsibility.

As I had lost a large area of skin from my arm, our First Aid expert advised iodine and promptly poured the contents of a bottle of this diabolical stuff on my arm with an effect something like being struck by lightning – and I passed out. Eventually coming round I was in time to hear a voice say, 'I can't feel his pulse' – which had me worried. Actually such tumbles were extremely rare and in the course of 400,000 miles of travel I cannot recall any serious accidents involving either myself or other riders although our rides involved not just country lanes, but rough moorland crossings, bridle ways, Alpine passes and so on. Surely, cycling must be the safest pastime of all.

Church Services, Dinners, etc.

Our members have taken part in various church services through the years, mainly in the thirties. Humbleton, Garton, Selby, Sigglesthorne, South Dalton and Beverley Minster come to mind. These generally took place on Armistice Sunday, but by far the best known and best attended has been that held at Coxwold annually since 1928 and traditionally in May. Although organised by the Teesside DA the Hull DA has always been closely involved with a strong contingent even though this meant a round trip of 120 miles for those making the journey within the day. Gill and Marie Gilleard have attended every year until recently.

Apart from the war years when the annual dinner was held out of town at such places as Kirkburn (Four Winds), Driffield (Bell Hotel) and even Cottingham (Brocklesbys), favoured dinner establishments were Powolneys (Hull) or the Beverley Arms, whilst occasional dances were held locally – I believe at the old Metropole Dance Hall in West Street.

Coxwold Church Service (1955).

Of outside events, Rabbit Pie suppers were very popular, usually held on New Year's Eve either at the Wellington Inn at Lund or Mrs Crompton's at Middleton-on-the-Wolds. I remember we used to form a circle in the roadway at some distance from the chosen venue and as the church bells welcomed the new year, we all sang 'Auld Lang Syne'.

Then there were those cycling Christmases. Two which immediately come to mind were based on the Bay Horse (Pateley Bridge) and Wass Grange Farm near Bylands Abbey. It was at Wass Grange that occurred the only occasion that the Hardriders were defeated by a meal! Normally they ate everything in sight, indeed, many were the times when, on the appearance of a replenished plate of eatables, the entire contents vanished before it reached the table! Well, on the occasion that we had our Christmas dinner at Wass, we were honoured by taking our meal with the farmer and his wife, the latter presiding at the festive table. Following our fifty-mile ride, we had developed a first class appetite and fondly imagined we could devour anything that might be put before us – but some of us may have had doubts when the turkey arrived. It was gigantic; in fact, I wasn't at all sure that it wasn't an ostrich! Then, of course, there were in addition, all the usual accessories which in themselves would have fed an army. By the time we had done what was expected of us with that lot, we were beginning to wonder how on earth we were going to cope with whatever was to follow. Then, into the room, to our utter amazement, was trundled the biggest Christmas pudding there ever was. It must have been twelve inches across and was completely spherical – a real picture book pudding. However, game to the last, the assembled Hardriders set to with a will, although it soon became apparent that, at last, they had met their Waterloo!

Then to round off a wonderful day, we all enjoyed a jolly good tramp over the frosted hills under a brilliant clear moon.

Clothing and Equipment

What did we wear in those early days? When I joined the club most of the riders wore some sort of knee breeches with perhaps a tweed jacket. Later plus-fours became fashionable, but at the same time shorts were beginning to appear. First the shorts would be khaki drill (ex army?) although later more sophisticated shorts became available – the principal supplier was, I think, the Hebden Cord Company. Particularly in the thirties, shorts and ankle socks became regulation wear, at any rate with

At Spurn Head (1930). Left to right: George Reeder, 'Pip' Pudsey, 'Skid' Colman, Syd Scruton, Alf Reeder, Percy Warrener, Ken Hughes, George Hope, 'Casey' Redfern, Ruby Hope, Noel Baker and C. P.

the Hardriders – even in the depth of winter. I can remember having my knees cased in ice with no ill effects. I used to argue that knees were not affected by cold conditions. Hands and feet, yes – but not knees.

In the warmer weather a light jacket of cotton or alpaca was usual, with pullovers available if required. Like the men, the ladies didn't seem to have any particular form of dress, the most usual being a longish coat with matching dress and thick woollen stockings. Sometimes this was varied by breeches and later, like the men, with plus fours.

For wet weather (it did rain sometimes), then as now, there seemed to be nothing to beat the cape – which had to be of fairly ample proportions. I think Barbours of South Shields were the favourite suppliers. But why had the cape to be black?

As for saddle bags (vital necessities), these had to be fairly roomy, particularly for the camper when it would be augmented by pannier bags. My first bag was an old canvas camera case of my father's, which initially seemed admirable though it soon became apparent that the makers didn't have cycle touring in mind when they had produced it many years previously, for it soon became the worse for wear. Now the Unit pigskin bag had appeared and two or three of our most discerning members had purchased them, so imagine my delight when my elder brother, knowing my predicament, bought me one. I really felt that I had 'arrived' even if my cycle was blue!

As far as I remember my first lamp was oil fuelled. These oil lamps produced a surprisingly good illumination, though they had to receive regular maintenance by cleaning, wick trimming etc. But it was essential not to turn the wick up too much in an endeavour to produce a better light as if this was done it had the effect of smoking up and completely blacking out the front glass. Now the first thing a policeman did when he stopped a cyclist for riding without a light was to clap his hand on the lamp to see if it was still hot. If cold it wasn't a scrap of use saying it had just gone out. These were the days when policemen had legs! Proud was the possessor of a Lucas King of the Road!

I was rather too late for the candle lamp era, but following on the oil lamp there were many interesting ones such as the acetylene, either with an integral water container or with this as a separate item connected to the lamp by a rubber tube. We mustn't overlook the dynamo lighting unit. This was either tyre-operated or built into the hub, usually the front, while the ever-popular battery lamp seems to go on forever. By the way, can anyone tell me why the batteries only last a fraction of the time they did pre-war?

Cycling Humour

Although cycle tourists, as a rule, took their pastime serious, club runs were quite happy occasions with a great deal of banter and wise-cracking. There were many humorous incidents, although the subtlety of the occasion might not have been apparent to a non-cyclist. However, on one occasion when riding somewhere near North Grimston, one of our party who always had a word for anyone or anything we passed, called out to a horse standing with its head hanging over a field gate. 'Good morning,' he called and to everyone's astonishment the reply came back in good old East Yorkshire dialect: 'Morning.' Unknown to us a farm worker had been in the field, obscured by the hedge – he probably thought what a friendly lot these cyclists are!

But humour can take various forms and what can be hysterically funny to one person can leave another cold. Take Albert Weaver's case, for instance. Now Albert was probably the best dressed member of the club, the only cyclist I knew who wore a tie, and on the occasion of our run to Kirkdale he turned up at the start in a magnificent, brand new, plus four suit of a rich plum colour. Well, we arrived at Kirkdale and after we had visited the tiny church, St. Gregory's Minster, and inspected the ancient sundial which is said to be of Saxon origin and to date back to 1055, it was decided to look at the cave, where, it was said, the bones of an elephant and suchlike prehistoric animals had been found in the dim and distant past. Complete with cycle lamps we entered the cave, which entailed crawling on our bellies for some distance, but despite the damp and mud, Albert, in true Hardriders spirit, came with us. On emerging Albert really was a sight for sore eyes, plastered as he was with yellow sticky mud – his beautiful suit ruined!

Jack Curl was well known in grass track racing circles in the thirties, competing in the 'flapper meetings' as they were called. However, I next met Jack in the sixties when we were both members of the Hull Ciné Club. It was then that Jack decided to augment his physical activities by investing in a 'home trainer'. Unfortunately, space was limited in the Curl household and the attic was the only place for it. Some of you may be aware of the volume of noise created as the cycle wheels rotated the large rollers – especially in a confined space. So as Jack steadily increased the tempo the resulting noise was quite horrendous. Next morning after the initial run he was greeted by his elderly neighbour with: 'Good morning, Jack – did you hear the thunder last night?' I am afraid there has been a lot of thunder in the neighbourhood since then.

Perhaps not in the same category of humour we have the many
adherents of the fixed wheel, a device used not only for propulsion but
for another purpose. Some would boast that by applying backward pressure on the pedals, they could 'hold in' on any hill – and didn't need a
brake! Sad to say I heard of more than one who didn't succeed, and as
the cycle rapidly took charge they finally 'bit the dust'! To see the cycle
increasingly taking charge really was funny!

I suppose the following is not, strictly speaking, humour, but here
goes anyway.

I had been enjoying one of my lone winter evening rides when, a
few miles out of Beverley on the Cherry Burton Road, I became aware
of a rattling sound behind me. Thinking at first that there must be
something loose on the cycle, I dismounted and 'bounced' the cycle on
the road, which should have indicated the cause. But all appeared perfectly
sound, so, puzzled, I remounted and continued my ride. However, the
rattle immediately resumed whilst, at the same time, I felt a chilling
sensation down my back. After a hundred yards or so, the rattle appeared
to leave me and veer across the road, whilst I heard a sound, as of cycle
tyres crunching over gravel, even as the rattle ceased. Going back to
investigate I found the gravel leading to a field gate! When I mentioned
this occurrence to the club members later, Syd Scruton, a Beverley man,
said that a short time previously a cyclist had been killed at the Cherry
Burton crossroads! So there we are.

Since the thirteenth century, Hull Fair, said to be the largest in the
country, has been held annually, except when it was cancelled in the
seventeenth century owing to the plague. But surely one of the most
hilarious occasions occurred one night in 1926 when a party of Hull
Thursday Road Club racing lads took over the bicycle roundabout!

This consisted of about a dozen bicycles, mounted in a circular formation and relying on the cycling prowess of the customers for propulsion.
These Thursday lads soon worked up a tremendous rate of knots, so
much so that the whole outfit developed a rhythmic shudder which
increased until the whole contraption was rocking violently, in distinct
danger of collapsing altogether. The method of stopping the roundabout,
when the customer's allotted time had expired, was to apply a brake,
which was operated by an attendant who was positioned inside the circle
of whirring bicycles. Needless to say, owing to the speed of the gyrating
bicycles by this time, it was impossible to stop it, so the lads probably
had the longest ride in history!

Some Memorable Rides

On Sunday runs we frequently visited the North Yorkshire moors – our 'happy hunting ground' – and we were especially keen on moorland crossings such as Wheeldale when the carrying of cycles was often the order of the day. This was, of course before the thousands of Lyke Wake walkers came on the scene! Then there was Bransdale, Rosedale, Baysdale, Ryedale, Farndale and Newtondale to say nothing of Goathland, Reivaulx, Black Hambleton, Beck Hole, Glaisdale and Robin Hood's Bay. Robin Hood's Bay: that brings to mind 'Windy Sunday' – who on that ride will ever forget it? When was it? The early thirties, I should think. We had ridden up by way of the Wolds, crossed the Vale of Pickering and cycled up Forge Valley on to Harwood Dale before turning off beyond the Flask Inn. By a track we descended by Stoupe Beck to the coast, from where we took to the sands as far as Robin Hood's Bay for lunch. We had been aware of a strong southerly wind as we rode north and by the time we reached Robin Hood's Bay it was obviously strengthening but we had encountered strong winds before and were not unduly worried. We climbed the hill out of Robin Hood's Bay but when we gained the open moor and turned our wheels southward we realised that we were for it. The wind had, by now, risen to something in the nature of a howling gale as we crawled along on our bottom gears. We will draw a veil over our journey home, recollection of which time has mercifully dimmed to some extent, but I do remember descending Cloughton Bank, normally the occasion for a wonderful downward swoop, but which on this occasion saw us reduced to struggling *down* on our bottom gears. We reached Driffield at about midnight and finally staggered in home along with the milk.

Who, of those involved will forget the Hardriders run in 1931 which included sixteen hours of continuous heavy rain! Now that really was an occasion. We had left home about midnight and after crossing the Wolds had made our way over the Moors for our pre-arranged breakfast at Guiseborough up near Saltburn. The establishment where we had breakfast had an adjoining bakery and the proprietor very kindly turned on the heating in the ovens and stowed all our wet garments, socks, shoes – the lot – so that by the time we were ready to take to the road once again the whole lot was done to a turn. What luxury to start off with nice warm garments!

We had always assumed that Sutton Bank in North Yorkshire was unclimbable – and so it was until the day in 1930 when Percy Warrener showed us that that was no longer the case. Percy showed us the way and it wasn't long before we were all climbing this notorious hill; if not with ease, at any rate we got up!

In those days Sutton Bank often defeated the efforts of even motorists to get their vehicles to the top and it was usual for a group of spectators to assemble in the hope of seeing some unfortunate motorist getting into

A change of exercise.

A spot of bother.

difficulties. What their thoughts were when the Hardriders rode up the hill in 'Club Formation' (that is, two by two) is not known.

But did we have any lady members of the Hardriders? Well, yes. Apart from Marie Gilleard, an original Hardrider, who ceased section riding quite early on, we had Gladys Bradley who later married Ken Dibnah, and Elsie Godfrey who, I believe, married another Hardrider, Bob Newmarch. Both these two were very accomplished riders and I have no recollection of either ever being 'dropped' – or did we seem more gentlemanly as time went by? Like so many riders, we seemed to lose track of both of them during the war.

Of other outstanding rides there was that ride to attend the Meriden Church Service. All our DAs and other clubs had contributed to build the grey granite obelisk on Meriden Green in memory of all the cyclists who had lost their lives during the First World War. It was in 1921 that the memorial was unveiled but our trip didn't take place until 1933 when Ken Hughes and I took our tandem on this run which saw 307 miles accounted for in the day.

Then there was the marvellous all-night ride in the course of which we made the Fleet Moss crossing from Wharfedale, climbing up to 1,857 feet on that great upland region which saw us over into Wensleydale.

I suppose I should tell you about that ride to Morecambe. How on earth did it come about? – Morecambe doesn't sound like our sort of destination! Well, when I first joined the club there was much talk of a former member famous for his prodigious rides, the ace being a ride to Morecambe and back – in a day. When I mentioned this to my partner on many runs and tours, Eric Charles, he said, 'We could do that.' Up to that point I hadn't given it a thought – I mean – Morecambe! However, the upshot was that on 21 June 1931 Eric and I were on our way westward, initially by that oh-so-familiar route by York, Ilkley, Skipton and Clapham. We had left Clapham and were crossing the Bentham Moor with about 120 miles under our belts, when Eric braked to a standstill and, to my surprise, announced that he was afraid he couldn't make it, suggesting that I continued to Morecambe and, by arrangement, picked him up on the way back. We had been ploughing against a strong head wind all night (my diary note states 'terrific westerly wind') so perhaps it wasn't surprising that he was feeling the strain. Anyhow, I agreed with Eric's suggestion and we both sat down and consumed some food, following which we both got on our cycles and continued the ride without another word being said about 'packing'. You see, what Eric had needed was food.

He was a truly remarkable fellow – not a regular cyclist at all. He played football during the winter and, after being off his cycle for months, would ring me and suggest an all-night ride – which meant two hundred miles or so. He was one of those incredibly fit individuals – he didn't seem to need any training! The ride continued to Lancaster, then on to Morecambe. Now I have no time for seaside resorts, and Morecambe was one of the last places on earth I would choose to be, so we simply rode as far as the sea front and, without getting off our cycles, simply rode out again. Realising that we would have that powerful westerly wind behind us we decided to make a ride of it by returning by way of Lancaster, Ingleton, Kingsdale, Dent, Garsdale and the usual run through Wensleydale – a much pleasanter route than that of the outer run. Anyway, exactly twenty-four hours after leaving home we were back with 263 miles to our credit.

Perhaps the most memorable of all was the run to High Cup Nick in August 1934. As was usual when tackling a long haul, we rode through the night and made Barnard Castle for breakfast by way of Scotch Corner. Following the Tees we then proceeded by way of Middleton-in-Teesdale as far as Langdon Beck where we left the road, already at a height of 1,250 feet and, with a ten mile trek before us, struck off south-west by the infant Tees as far as Cauldron Snout. From here we followed the Maize Beck over the moors, reaching the 2,000-feet mark. From there the stupendous High Cup Nick was revealed to us. The 'nick', a great cleft in the surrounding fells, plunged 800 feet down to High Cup Beck threading its way far below. A never-to-be-forgotten experience. But our day wasn't done and after descending to Dufton we continued to Appleby for a well-earned tea. With tea out of the way we continued to Kirkby Stephen and Nateby before turning eastward for wonderful Birkdale Common. Although by now it was pitch dark the glorious swoop down to Keld was pure magic and soon we were in Muker where we had booked accommodation at Mrs Kilburn's Swale Farm. As it was a bank holiday the farmhouse was full up but we had been allocated beds in the village. It seemed that nearly everyone was in bed but eventually our little party were assembled and, with a guide carrying a hurricane lamp, we were marched off to our beds. It was then a matter of 'two in here' 'one in here' and so on. Swale Farm was a famous CTC house for many years and Mrs Kilburn a highly regarded host. She died a few years ago aged more than a hundred.

Now Mrs Kilburn had a daughter who lived up at Crackpot Hall near Swinner Gill and, following a visit to her mother at Muker, would walk back home by way of a riverside path through a lonely valley flanked by the 1,600 feet Kisdon Hill on one side and Black Hill on the other.

She often did the journey at night. When arriving home she would, by arrangement, signal her safe arrival by displaying a lamp which would be visible at the three-mile distant Muker! Crackpot Hall is, regrettably, now a ruin.

Despite my enthusiasm for cycling there were times when, either alone or with others, I abandoned my cycle and took to two feet. I always regarded walking as the next best thing to cycling. I didn't take my cycle up Ben Nevis nor up Helvellyn but I did wear cycling shoes!

War Clouds Gather

Our last major tour, before the war, never got off the ground. We had planned to go to the Pyrenees and Andorra and, although war was imminent, we decided, optimists that we were, to travel down to London to check the possibilities of getting to Perpignan, which was to be the starting point of our tour. The party was made up of Cyril Andrews, Cliff Arndt (of Sheffield), Tom Clayton, Jim Crozier (Liverpool), Norman Wilson (Liverpool) and myself. Well, we got to London all right, but at Victoria Station we were told that there was no possibility of getting beyond Paris. Obviously this was a blow, but not being prepared to give in without a fight, we decided to ride on to Newhaven and talk to passengers coming off the Dieppe boat.

As, I suppose, we half expected, there was no encouragement there, as we were told that conditions in France were absolutely chaotic! That did it – so we decided to spend the next week or so in Devon. It was a great disappointment, but we were determined to make the best of a bad job, and for several days things continued fairly normally, except that several catering establishments, fearing food rationing, were rather difficult about supplying food! Events took rather a grim turn when, a few days later in Brixton, we learned that Poland had been invaded and it looked as if nothing could prevent a war. Sure enough, we heard the sad news whilst in the Cheddar Gorge. There seemed to be nothing for it but to head home. And that was how our 1939 tour started – and finished.

We heard later that when news of the declaration of war was announced on the radio, a party of cyclists at Mrs Crompton's tea house were made to stand to attention and sing God Save the King.

2

Bicycle Polo

It was on one of Harry Wharton's annual trips to London, primarily to attend the 'Best All-Rounder' concert at the Albert Hall, that I was first introduced to Bicycle Polo. On the day following the concert we attended a general sports meeting at the old Crystal Palace, where the main attraction was a demonstration Bicycle Polo match between two of London's crack teams which created the spark that made me realise that this was the game we needed up north. (Incidentally, the Crystal Palace was burned down soon after our visit.) On returning home I at once started making enquiries regarding suppliers of equipment, rules etc., and in this George Brake, the National Secretary of the Bicycle Polo Association, was of considerable help. Later, George brought his team, the Wren Wheelers, up to Hull where we met them in a friendly match on Jackson's playing field on Inglemire Lane. We learned in that one game more than we could ever have done merely playing among ourselves. One lesson was that the game couldn't be played half-heartedly – you had to throw all your effort and ability into it. After that game I was hooked and soon other local clubs became interested, though it must be said that, initially, there was a certain amount of reluctance. Inevitably, as I started it all, I was landed with the secretary's job! The teams involved were, apart from the CTC, Hull Thursday Road Club, Hull Clarion (a well-supported club in those days), Reindeer, (later Phoenix before expiring altogether), and Newland (this was a pure Bicycle Polo club), but several clubs provided two teams. Quickly a league was established and thrived until the war brought it all to a halt, although soon after we had made a start the game had taken root in many northern towns and cities, joining the Derby Clarion and the London clubs, who had been playing for some time. Apart from our own League games we played at Liverpool, Manchester, Newcastle, Leeds and London with a certain amount of success; we also formed a Yorkshire team.

Those who appeared in the CTC team included: Harry Wharton (Captain), Charlie Barker, Arthur Batty, Bill Boards, Ken Hughes, Norman Skelton, Dicky Smith, Bunny Stephenson, Frank and Harry Suddaby and myself, whilst other CTC members who played a vital part in the success of the league included Bob Craggy, a very capable referee, and Tom Garniss who, as well as refereeing, also made a film of our activities.

At the York Rally. Left to right: Harry Suddaby, Bunny Stephenson, Frank Suddaby, Joe Gosling, Arthur Grant, and Tim King.

Action at the York Rally.

Harry Wharton (Captain) of Hull CTC. receives the Championship Cup.
Others (standing) Arthur Batty and Ken Hughes
(below) C.P., Dicky Smith and Bob Craggy.

Although it is fifty-five years since those pre-war polo days, I do remember the names of some who were prominent with other clubs. Hull Thursday Road Club included Joe Gosling, Arthur Grant, Tim King and Jack McGlone, and for Clarion there were George Edmonds, Larry Johnson, Les Newby, Len Noble, Ken Scott and Bill Walker. I am afraid most of the names have faded from memory, but there were Reindeer members Ernie Thompson and Tommy Toalster. Incidentally, Larry Johnson later became prominent as a City Councillor and, indeed, still is. He was Lord Mayor a few years ago.

Our early league games were played at Eppleworth, and I remember our first game there, when the ground had a covering of snow! We must have had advance warning of the snow as we came armed with a red ball. Later games were played at Dunswell, which was where the game finally petered out with the outbreak of war. The CTC team won most of their games initially (often by a 'cricket score'), but other teams made good progress and, in the final year before the war, we shared the championship with the Hull Thursday Road Club.

In the early days our equipment was, I suppose, rather primitive! To achieve a cycle which roughly resembled the real thing the following procedure was adopted. Acquiring an old frame the front forks were straightened out, thus greatly shortening the wheelbase, while at the same time a 24th fixed sprocket was fitted to achieve the necessary ultra-low gear. This conversion produced a cycle which was quickly manoeuvrable and with the low gear, capable of rapid acceleration. No brakes were permitted, of course. Later, wheels were rebuilt with tandem gauge spokes, although by this time some riders had acquired 'pukka' polo cycles.

3

Cycling in Wartime

The twenties and particularly the thirties were undoubtedly the golden days for the DA, (as, indeed, it was for the club itself), with a host of activities and membership climbing to five hundred. The 1939 edition of the splendidly compiled DA Handbook, produced by the joint editors Eddie Rayner and Tom Webster, proved to be the last as, with war looming, the membership was sadly depleted as the forces claimed more and more of our members, and others were sent by their firms to branches in other parts of the country – to supposed safety! However, although only a skeleton of its former self, the DA kept going with a programme of runs, whilst the clubroom was as popular as ever. Harry Wharton provided a greatly appreciated facility through his News Letter, through which he kept in touch with all known members in the forces. Harry was one of the founder members of the DA as was A.F. 'Gill' Gilleard and his wife Marie. Gill was the DA Treasurer for a considerable number of years whilst Marie was the original Social Secretary. Mainly through Harry's News Letter, we were able to keep in touch with over fifty members serving in the forces. Of other members, still at home, many were associated with various Air Raid Precaution services, including the cyclists' messenger service, which had been established in Hull in common with certain other cities. Jack Collier was the divisional officer for East Hull, whilst I took Central Hull and Ida was deputy DO in West Hull where Tim King of the Hull Thursday Road Club was in charge. Another HTRC member, Harrold Sykes, looked after North Hull.

Much has been written about the air raids on Hull, perhaps the most bombed city outside London, although referred to only as a 'north-east town' on the radio.

I suppose many have their own narratives to relate of the dreadful happenings of those days. For myself, leaving the more horrific aspects on one side, I recall two particular incidents.

On one occasion, during a blitz, we became aware of an aircraft firmly locked in the mesh of a dozen searchlights. Assuming this to be an enemy aircraft, all and sundry were rejoicing, although all that was knocked on the head when it was learned next day that the plane that came down in the Dunswell area was actually 'one of ours'. Although it occurred during a blitz, my other recollection had a humorous side to it. With the air filled with the drone of enemy aircraft and searchlights probing the sky whilst the crump of bombs mingled with the sound of anti-aircraft fire, the assembly was almost entirely concerned with the air raid. All, that is, except an old air raid warden, known to be a keen horticulturalist, obviously with his thoughts far away from the war, who suddenly turned to me and said, ' 'ev yer tatties got blight?'

Ida and I were married in May 1943. We didn't tell anyone, except Harry Wharton who was my best man, as I hated anything in the nature of a 'public performance', especially as, with my mother seriously ill, it didn't seem appropriate. We went to the church on a Claud Butler tandem and afterwards had a few days with Eddie and Molly Green at Near Sawrey in the Lake District. Ida later got permission to transfer her job to the cycle trade which was an enormous help.

But what was it like cycling in war-time? Well, the most noticeable feature, and one in which cyclists truly rejoiced, was the rapidly diminishing volume of traffic. It is true that the traffic density of pre-war roads hardly compared with the present day. Nevertheless the traffic had been steadily mounting throughout the thirties, pedestrian crossing were introduced and there was much talk of the need for by-passes for some of the villages. Some of us kept up a steady barrage of correspondence, through the press, concerning road safety matters in connection with cyclists and motorists during this period. But with the war, there was a vast improvement, particularly from a cyclist's point of view. The absence of traffic we applauded and even the complete removal of sign posts really wasn't a deterrent, even while touring in strange areas – perhaps it made us better map readers! I certainly cannot recall getting into difficulties, although we toured in Wales and the Lake District. We should like to have gone up to the Scottish Highlands but this area was out of bounds.

As the Whitsuntide holiday approached in 1940 there was much talk of the likely invasion by Hitler, but nevertheless we decided that we should take the opportunity for a tour in the Dales. Now it may not have seemed an ideal occasion to plan an all-night ride but we wanted to continue our activities as normally as possible – perhaps, at the back of our minds, we wondered if this might be our last tour.

Our little party comprised Bunny Stephenson, Tom and Muriel Garniss together with Cyril Garner of Huddersfield, who met us later, and of course myself. We proceeded by way of North Newbald to Market Weighton but before reaching the latter we were stopped by a party of soldiers who, after examining our identity cards, questioned us as to why we were out cycling in the middle of the night. Our explanation that we liked cycling at night was greeted with disbelief. We were allowed to proceed but were stopped again and again. The further we got from the coast the less our appearance on the scene seemed to be of concern, but the night really went without further incident, though on passing Barmby Moor we did listen for our corncrake who had previously invariably greeted us from a nearby field as we passed by. He wasn't there and we never heard him again.

The only incident during the rest of our tour occurred while crossing the Redmire Firing Range next afternoon. We noted from the indicator that no firing was imminent so commenced the long climb to the summit with clear minds. However, we had just reached the top and were commencing the descent when there was an almighty burst of gun fire. So great was our fear of being shot off our cycles that we set off like bats out of hell, achieving what must have been the fastest time ever for that descent! Casualties – nil.

Cycling, apart from the usual Sunday runs, was rather restricted for obvious reasons, but Ida and I did manage to squeeze in a few days in North Wales in 1944 when Harry Johnson told us of some accommodation which was still available there. It was a relief to get away from the constant atmosphere of war, which in Hull seemed to be so very close. In Wales you could have imagined the war to be a million miles away because of the beauty of the countryside and even the demeanour of the people. Of course we couldn't help hearing odd snatches of happenings in the war – nearly always unpleasant.

Of course club runs continued, even though with reduced attendances. However, it was a joy to get away into the clean air of the countryside after the week's close association with the war, air raids and so on. But it wasn't always so, for part of the Wolds area, especially around Wetwang, was used as a tank training ground which certainly made you keep your eyes peeled as tanks were liable to burst suddenly through the hedge – cross the road – and disappear through the hedge opposite (more hedges existed in those days). One had to watch the hedgeside even more than the road! Many of our catering houses ceased to function, but one of the few that did, and which provided a greatly appreciated service, was Brambledene. Mrs Crighton had lived in the middle of what became the Pocklington Airfield, her house being, of course, requisitioned before she transferred to Brambledene. Another of our ports of call was the Black Swan at Wetwang which became a favourite haunt of the Free French stationed nearby. And a right lively lot they were – we quite enjoyed our visits there whilst some were able to polish up their French!

I mentioned earlier that I was not interested in the racing game.

However, it was during the war that I took part in my one and only racing activity. The Hull Thursday Road Club, of which I was a member, was the only local racing club still active owing to the inevitable reduced membership, attendances at events were falling alarmingly so when some of us were asked to augment the numbers by taking part in a 25-mile Time Trial . . . well, we agreed.

But what about cycling at night? Of course, we never thought of restricting our rides and cycling during the hours of darkness. Our partially blacked-out lamps and the eerie sensation of riding through villages with everything completely blacked-out, was a strangely fascinating experience. But Ida and I were involved in a rather alarming incident on one occasion. Returning from a ride we found when we approached the level-crossing in Northgate (Cottingham) that the gates were closed for an approaching train. Now the usual procedure for a cyclist in such circumstances was to cross the line by the pedestrian gate, after checking that the train was far enough away for safety, or course. Well, we went through the gate, and, as the coast was clear, started to cross the line – but then it happened. Apparently, in the pitch darkness, Ida stepped off the crossing and onto the track – lost her footing and went down with her cycle on top of her – pinning her down. Talk about panic! Somehow or other I managed to get Ida to her feet and transferred to safety, while, with seconds to spare I rescued the two cycles, as the train came hurtling down the line. Phew! Ida had dislocated her shoulder which meant a trip to hospital, but it could have been so much worse.

Another war-time incident may appear very amusing now, but at the time it could have been disastrous. I had read in *Cycling* that 'on being attacked by a dog the cyclist should hold the inflator [pump] by the bottom end and direct it violently towards the offending animal, which would be so scared by the suddenly extending inflator that it was unlikely to offend again'. Now, on returning home from the shop, I was frequently attacked by a nasty little Scottie at a certain spot so I thought I'd put this advice into practice. Right on schedule the Scottie attacked, so, as advised, I whipped out my pump and lashed out at the offending pup. It worked like a charm as the pump extended to the utter amazement of the dog, but unhappily at the same time out shot the *connection* which disappeared into the shrubbery of a nearby garden. I should have mentioned that during the war certain accessories were almost impossible to obtain and one of these so necessary items was the pump connection! It will be appreciated that my disappearing pump connection just had to be found. So I had the humiliating experience of crawling around in that garden in search of my missing treasure!

Another 'doggy' incident occurred while descending a steep hill in Castle Howard Park. I shot through one of those gate-houses which obliterate the view beyond, but on emerging, a huge dog, which I swear was a big as a donkey, chose that precise moment to cross the road. I hit him, but as my cycle was brought to a violent halt I was pitched clean over the handlebars! So great was my momentum that I landed on my feet, kept my balance, and continued up the road with enormous strides! I take no credit for this feat – it just happened! But what happened to the dog? Well, to the best of my knowledge, he's still running!

4

The Shop

Prewar

I suppose 1934 must be regarded as one of my most important years for that was when Frank Suddaby and I entered the cycle business. Mind you, things were far from easy in the early days; even the finding of a suitable shop to make a start seemed hedged with difficulties, nearly making us give up the idea before we got started. In the end, however, we found a very much run down cycle shop, which the owner, through illness, had allowed to become very much neglected. This was at 84 Spring Bank. But our troubles were not over as a capital of £160 (£80 each) really wasn't enough, even in 1934, whilst, owing to the immediate piling up of expenses, we dared not take out more than £1 per week each, though after a while we did give ourselves a rise of 10 shillings (50p)! Soon however, with fair support from the club lads, we did enjoy a slow but sure build-up of customers, enabling us to get our feet on the ground. But to me it seemed oh, so slow – but then I always was an impatient sort!

I should have mentioned that when Frank and I started at the shop we were really rather 'green', with little knowledge of business, nor of the many things, including repairs, which we were expected to tackle. True, we were experts at mending punctures, but you can't make a living out of mending punctures. However, we were quick to learn and soon we were amazing ourselves at what we accomplished. Indeed it wasn't long before we built our first frame. To accomplish this we had to call on my brother Eric, who had taken lessons in brazing while at the Technical College. We first dissected an old frame to see how the tubes were brazed together, then we prepared drawings and away we went! Our technique was polished up as we went along. Later, the lads used to bring us their specifications, incorporating notions of their own. It pleased them that they had designed their own frames, but the truth is that often their specifications didn't work out and we had to build the frames as they should be – without saying anything. We built quite a few frames but beyond polishing and generally finishing the metalwork, we had to send the frames out for enamelling and plating. Then of course, along came the war to put a damper on things.

Saturday morning.

In those pre-war days, there were said to be 140 cycle dealers in Hull, but this figure must have included many half-hearted dealers who only regarded cycles as a side line. Of those who might be said to be 100% concerned with 'our' side of the trade were Jack Kirk, Parker Walker, Len Noble and George Robinson, whilst other prominent general purpose dealers included Stevens, Jordans, Horsley, Saner, Corden and Smithson.

The Shop in Wartime

Quite early in the hostilities Frank left me to return to sea. He had been a merchant seaman before joining me in the cycle shop, so I suppose it was the natural thing for him to do. He made rapid strides and quickly gained his master's ticket with his own command. While on leave during the war he used to stay with me — his parents having evacuated to Pateley Bridge — and he used to surprise me when air-raids were on by saying he would have felt safer were he at sea!

I had a youngster helping me and we seemed to be working all hours on cycle repairs, when, rather than let anyone down, I would as often as not work until the early hours of the morning. Ida used to come in to help in the shop after leaving her job in a coal merchant's office. Actually, she wanted to join the Land Army, but it seems that her job in the coal merchant's office was thought to be more important, just as was my work repairing 'the workers'' cycles! Incredibly, despite the vast amount of damage the air-raids brought to the city, the shop managed to escape without a scratch. Was Hitler a cyclist?

It was during the war that, on the death of the owner of the property, I was able to purchase the premises at the ensuing auction (my first experience of an auction!). Then, at about the same time, on the advice of our accountant, the business was turned into a limited company.

We had a constant problem obtaining stock for re-sale and had we relied on the local suppliers I don't think we would have survived. As it was we had dealings with several out-of-town wholesalers, who helped out. On one occasion we had a trip down to Birmingham with fair success. But in those strange days you didn't order specific items but just left it to the supplier to send anything that could be remotely considered as saleable! We certainly accumulated a lot of rubbish.

We were involved in a remarkable incident in the middle of the war. We received a rare delivery of cycles. These came from Carltons of Worksop and the arrival of the six crated cycles coincided with the arrival of a party of American Air Force men, who were stationed across in Lincolnshire but often visited us. Seeing the cycles they insisted on the crates being opened up so they could inspect the cycles. Well, imagine the scene – there were only two of us and it was some task uncrating the cycles which then had to be unwrapped, pedals fitted etc. Whilst this was going on the Yanks were selecting which cycles they wanted, whilst we had to attend to any other customers who happened to drop in. So all the cycles had to be checked over, and in most cases additional accessories fitted. As each cycle was completed it was taken outside for a trial run, before being returned for adjustments to bars, saddles etc. What a day, but it was great fun – and good business, as a delivery of cycles was extremely rare. One chap bought six rear lamps which had to be fitted to the rear stays – what a sight. By the time all had been supplied they had been taken out and ridden up and down Spring Bank, although it didn't seem to matter which side of the road they were on!

1945–1972

With the war behind us the business was able to go forward. Frank had returned from sea and at the time seemed glad to resume his pre-war activities while at the same time Bunny Stephenson joined us as a director on his release from the army. Then at the same time, my brother Noel, having spent years out in Burma with the army, threw in his lot with us to take charge of frame-building.

But it was obvious that we were far too cramped at Spring Bank for frame building on the scale we had in mind and we purchased Britannia House in Mytongate (this was quite a famous old building which years later survived the reconstruction which seemed to eliminate most of the surrounding property). With Mytongate under our belt, so to speak, we were able to install a sand-blasting plant, together with facilities for bonderising (a phosphating process to prevent rusting) which enabled us to do our own enamelling. When we started up in Mytongate Jackie Stather joined us to look after repairs and the shop which we established. Jackie, a member of the Hull Thursday Road and a keen road race participant, had regrettably lost a leg while with the army in the desert, but he wasn't going to be defeated and for a while took part in road races, despite his great handicap!

One good thing which came out of the war was the occasional availability of tools which the Americans sent across under the 'lease-lend' scheme. These were of excellent quality and I suppose many are still in use. These were found to be of especial help at Mytongate as British tools were hard to come by.

Things went pretty well at Mytongate and we turned out hundreds

of frames for racing and touring, but our 'ace' frame was undoubtedly
the lady's Twin-Lat in which we came to specialise. A touring frame,
the main feature was the pair of ½" tubes running direct from the head
to the rear end with no bends, the purpose being to provide a semi-open
frame, as required by most lady riders. This produced a very responsive
frame owing to the bracing effect of the twin stays, so very superior to
the normal 'whippy' lady's frame. We sent these frames to all parts of
the country and they were a big success. Some years later, inevitably,
the big manufacturers got on to the idea and produced their own version,
but so inferior.

We still had customers among the Americans as long as there were
bases in the vicinity and I well remember building a racing frame for a
chap based at Holme-on-Spalding-Moor. I remember this particularly
because his frame had to be 26" the largest frame possible with the tubing
available, and as he was about 6' tall, nothing else would do. Bunny and
I delivered the frame to the base, and there were entertained in the chap's
office (I don't know his rank). In the course of our visit he was called
out and hauled over the coals for entertaining visitors while wages were
being handled in the adjacent office.

C.P. display stand at the York Rally.

Frank never really settled down after the war and eventually he left us to return to sea, (where I am sure he belonged) and he continued with his own command until he retired.

Of course in the seriousness of running the business we did have humorous moments. There was the occasion when in the course of being shown the 'art' of brazing, Bunny became so intent on watching the process that he failed to notice where he was waving his brazing torch and managed to set my hair on fire!

But talking about fire reminds me of another occasion. My office was directly above the workshop so when I heard a great commotion going on below (no one thought to tell me what was happening) I went to investigate and found the workshop full of dense smoke in the centre of which was a *flaming bicycle*. Apparently a cycle, awaiting a repair job, had been accidentally pushed onto a combustion stove thus igniting the celluloid mudguards and the tyres with the inevitable result. At the moment I arrived Bunny was in the act of shoving the blazing cycle out through the side door and into the street. As he emerged amid much coughing and spluttering accompanied by a huge volume of black smoke which rolled across the road and up the wall opposite, a window-cleaner operating on an adjacent window remarked, without turning his head and as though this sort of thing happened all the time, 'Having a bit of a fire?'

All went reasonably well for many years although, to be honest, I wasn't entirely happy that all the effort which went into the Mytongate project was worthwhile so, when we were made an offer for the building by a firm of importers, we decided to let it go, but at the same time purchased a cycle shop on Hessle Road where Bunny took charge assisted by Ian Hourston.

It would be the mid-sixties that we took over Jack Kirk's shop in Ferensway. Jack himself had looked after the Ferensway shop, leaving George Hope in charge at the Newland Avenue shop, but after Jack died, George came to Ferensway until Mrs Kirk decided to sell – and so we established our third shop.

Things then ran fairly smoothly for a number of years but eventually I began to think of retiring and so began a period of 'shrinkage'. First we pulled out of Hessle Road (there was some talk of the property coming down anyway), and then with the lease on Ferensway running out and the Council putting a ridiculous figure on a possible renewal, we decided that that too should go. So we were then more or less back to where we had started thirty-eight years earlier.

Incidentally, our contemporaries on the club side of the cycle trade

Bryan, who has now taken over the business.

in the years between 1945 and 1972 were: The Cottingham Cycle Centre, Ken Ellerker, Doug Scott, Bert Stutt and Eric Suffill.

I decide to retire

But deciding to retire and actually doing so are two totally different things. Perhaps my chief worry at the time was what would happen to the business – I couldn't bear the thought that it might either cease to exist, or would become something quite contrary to my ideas. But to tell you the truth I was beginning to feel the strain, what with three shops and the continuing pressure of organizing the York Rally which had become, I must confess, something of an obsession, even though the club's headquarters had taken over some of the work. Yet I couldn't give it up. But I had made up my mind to retire and I must say that Ida was in full agreement with this as she too, who had supported me in all my activities, must also have had enough. In making the vital decision to call it a day, I told myself that things would be much more comfortable with only the York Rally, gardening, photography, cycling, and so on, to consider, and when at about this time Bryan Loukes expressed an interest in the shop I almost looked forward to the Great Day. Bryan had been with me for seventeen years and I had every confidence that with his enthusiasm and ability – well, he was the man for the job. So in 1972, after thirty-eight years I ceased to be a cycle dealer! But the business continued and though it was a limited company, Bunny and I relinquished our shares. I am pleased however to say that Bryan decided to retain the name. Bunny decided to work for Bryan as a mechanic until a year or so ago.

Bryan is making an undoubted success of the business and I feel sure that much of his success can be credited to the help and support he received from his wife Ada – just as I received the encouragement of Ida. Bryan is one of Raleigh's leading dealers, nationally and they often call on him for advice when contemplating a new model. Incidentally, Bryan's shop manager is John Osgerby, needless to say another cyclist, who takes a big part in the success of the Hull DA.

5

The National Council

In 1944 I was persuaded to stand for the National Council of which
Eddie Green, a very good friend of the DA, was already a member. In
agreeing to stand I reasoned that if, in the unlikely event of being elected,
I should take the vacant place, I should join up with Eddie (the Yorkshire
region was allocated two places at the time). Unfortunately things did
not work out as planned, for although I was elected, the other place
went, not to Eddie, but to W. T. Wardale of Sheffield. You see, although
Eddie was a highly respected member well known in various parts of the
country, he hailed from the Lake District with its limited number of
members, while W.T. Wardale came from Sheffield with its greater voting
strength. I was truly sorry about this, but it was too late to do a thing
about it.

*At the Parbold Rally (1949). Margaret Riddell, Ida Pratt, 'Winova' Williams,
Arnold Hall, Bert Williams, [unknown], Bob Riddell (Councillor for Yorkshire),
Bert Light (Councillor for Lancashire) Fred Longley (Councillor for Lancashire)
and [unknown].*

In Dovedale. Left to right: Arthur Smith (Councillor for Gloucestershire), Edwin Green (Councillor for Wales), Ida Pratt, and Bill Oakley (Chairman of the Council).

In January 1945, I attended my first Council meeting at the club's headquarters at No.3 Craven Hill, London. Wishing to be away from the shop for as little time as possible I travelled down to London on the night train and all went well as far as Doncaster where a change had to be made, with its consequent delay. The train I joined was packed almost to bursting point, mainly with soldiers and other service personnel either going on leave or returning. I had to stand almost the whole of the journey. From Doncaster the progress was of the 'Stop-Go' variety, but after a nightmare trip, London was approached. Then, just short of Wood Green, we came to a halt and all passengers were instructed to leave the train and make their way through Wood Green to the tube station, from where the journey to King's Cross would be completed. It transpired that a rocket bomb had landed nearby during an air raid which was still

progressing. The main line was put out of action while enormous damage had been done in Wood Green, though I never heard what casualties had occurred. Leaving the lights of the train behind I was faced with an immediate problem. My eyesight is particularly poor in darkness and I was almost helpless. Fortunately a soldier came to my rescue and piloted me through Wood Green, crunching our way over masses of broken glass, finally reaching the tube station. Reaching King's Cross I just had time to get a wash in time for the Council meeting.

By then I was beginning to wonder if this Council business was a good idea! Happily nothing so traumatic happened again during the remaining twenty-four years of my spell on the Council.

Attending meetings was, for me, quite a problem as it meant being away from the shop at the busiest time of the week. I owed a lot to Ida over this, but she never complained about being left, along with others, to hold the fort. Council meetings were held on Saturday mornings in such places as Birmingham, Blackpool, Bournemouth, Brighton, Cardiff, Edinburgh, Glasgow, Liverpool, Newcastle and Richmond as well as our own headquarters in London, of course, thus entailing a considerable amount of travelling – and one night away from home.

Meetings of the District Associations and General Purposes committee, of which I was a member – and later chairman – were held at the club's headquarters on Friday evenings, so in order to attend these meetings I travelled down to London on the Friday (this took the best part of a day in those days), and then returned home on the midnight train, which landed me home at about 5.30 a.m., allowing me a couple of hours' sleep before dashing off to the shop. On those occasions I usually met up with Bob Carmichael-Riddell of Leeds, my colleague on both the Council and the DA & GP committee.

Reluctantly, after twenty-four years' service, in 1969 I felt I had to give up the Council, as I felt that organising the York Rally, together with the expanding cycle business, was as much as I could cope with.

6

The York Rally

The rally originated from an idea from the Hull and East Riding District Association at a meeting of the DA committee on 18 December 1944, when C.A. Pratt raised the question of the possibilities of organising an annual inter-DA meet with the object of encouraging closer collaboration between neighbouring DAs. This led to a meeting held in York on 18 March 1945 when the Yorkshire Inter-DA Committee came into being. Those attending that meeting were Mrs. L. Bennett, R.G.M. Carmichael-Riddell, A. Fox and W. Firth (all of the Mid-Yorkshire DA) Mrs J. Brufton, E. Gill, H. Lancaster, and K.E. Stainton (Sheffield DA) L. Dawson, G. Jeffcote, F. Rowntree and G. Claxton-Smith (Teeside DA) Mrs C.A. Pratt, H.E. Harland, G.E. Munson, and C.A. Pratt (Hull & East Riding DA). In addition Mr. W.T. Wardale Councillor (of Sheffield) attended.

A simple decision was made to hold a rally 'in or near York' in July. I must say that there didn't appear to be a great deal of enthusiasm for the idea and I got the impression that in view of the enormous difficulties facing us, some didn't expect the event to get off the ground. To give an idea of the size of the event the committee visualised, a resolution was passed: 'Each DA be asked to donate ten shillings towards initial expenses', and this was solemnly carried. It was also decided that the title of the event should be 'The Grand All-Yorkshire Cyclists Rally'.

I won't dwell on the initial trials and tribulations facing us – and they were many – particularly finding a suitable ground. Goodness knows how many letters I wrote, to say nothing of the miles Ida and I rode in search of what was beginning to look like the impossible. But then out of the blue came a letter from the Town Clerk of York to say that he had misinterpreted his committee's earlier decision and would I let him have further particulars of our proposed event. The clouds had lifted! Our rally was on.

Now right from that never-to-be-forgotten Sunday in September 1945 when the very first York Rally was held on the beautiful Knavesmire, the event has proved to have tremendous appeal. The event was on nothing like the scale it was later to become, yet seemed to be accepted. Something that none of us had thought of was the fact that cyclists of varying interests were quite content to meet and talk cycling, in a cycling atmosphere.

Cyclists arriving at the rally.

The start of a track race.

The CTC stand at the York Rally.

Ron Kitching stand at the York Rally.

Touring Hazards Event.

*C.P. receives Championship shield from Peter Rowntree
on behalf of the Hull DA.*

G. H. Stancer
(Past President of the CTC).

We had arranged a programme of simple field events, the star attraction being a Bicycle Polo match, whilst facilities were provided for camping. A well known personality, Peter Rowntree, opened the proceedings whilst later speeches were delivered by the CTC National Secretary Nevill Whall and by Reg. C. Shaw, then Assistant Secretary and Editor of the *Gazette*. The committee had optimistically forecast an attendance of five hundred but were amazed, not to say embarrassed, when five thousand turned up.

The event was voted a great success so it was inevitable that the Rally had to be repeated in 1946. And the crowds came again and, in ever increasing numbers, continue to come annually right up to the present day. The rally, initially a one-day event, soon developed on more pretentious lines and in 1950, with the introduction of additional features, it covered both the Saturday and the Sunday.

The success of the event was a source of satisfaction to the committee as it was to me, but by 1954 I had to tell the Council that the work involved had become such that I simply couldn't cope. Various suggestions were made, such as sending a secretary up from headquarters to assist with correspondence etc., In the end, however, it was decided that headquarters would take over much of the administration, at the same time adopting the event as the official National Rally. The management was to be left in the hands of the original committee, whilst I would continue as organiser of the event including, of course, the Cycle Show which by then had greatly expanded and was an important part of the rally. It was then, with the event coming under the jurisdiction of the National

Welcome banner.

Council, that the name of the event became the York Rally – as it was always known anyway.

The Manufacturers and Traders Union was very concerned about the York Rally Cycle Show as they considered that it detracted from the attendance at their own annual show at Earls Court. So much did they regard this opposition that in 1948, on the occasion of the first AIT York Rally, they offered the club one hundred guineas on the condition that no show was held or permitted. Needless to say, this was declined, but later, they banned their members from showing at York. However, with

Family in camp.

the event growing in size and popularity, and on the insistence of the leading manufacturers who wished to exhibit their products, the ban was lifted and the two organisations became on more friendly terms.

But it all seemed to happen at York in 1948. A national newspaper, the *News Chronicle*, organised an event which required cyclists to record certain places visited on their way to York. That was all very well, but when they tried to claim the York Rally as their event, that could not be tolerated and I personally had no hesitation in dismantling their huge scaffolding which bore a sign referring to 'The News Chronicle York Rally'. As a result of this occurrence, the committee had no hesitation in making the decision never to seek, nor accept, sponsorship.

As the scope of the rally expanded new features and events were introduced and at once a popular success was the Saturday evening Travel Talks with well known cycling personalities presenting slide shows concerning cycle touring. Then there was the Sunday morning Special Cyclists' Service in the Minster, followed by a Grand Parade of cyclists on a variety of mounts, from penny- farthings to modern touring and racing machines – all creating a rare spectacle as they made their way through the streets of York from the Minster to the Knavesmire. Among the club's membership are many accomplished photographers and the

A section of the crowd.

Photographic Competition never fails to produce a fine batch of colour slides, whilst the map-reading experts are likewise provided with their own special event. Cycle rides in the lanes in the vicinity of York are arranged, whilst on the arena, roller-racing contests create considerable interest as does the parade of ancient cycles presented by the Yorkshire Bygone Bykes Club. Particularly popular among the numerous field events are the cycle grass track events, the parade of cycling families and the election of the Bicycle Belle.

Without doubt, the two principal rally features are the Camp and the Cycle Show. Like all features of the rally, the Camp started as a very modest affair with about half a dozen tents, but through the years has expanded until these days it provides a grand mile-long spectacle of colourful tents housing over two thousand campers.

Way back in 1947 came the introduction of the Cycle Show, when four Yorkshire cycle dealers – Ron Kitching (Harrogate), Arnold Elsegood (York), J.T. Rodgers (Frank Kennedy) (Leeds) and Cliff Pratt (Hull) pooled their stocks of what were then 'short supply' items of interest to club cyclists and put on a display in a small tent. This proved immensely popular and provided a sight for sore eyes with thousands of cyclists queuing for hours to parade through the tiny tent to gloat over these unpurchasable goods! But here again expansion was rapid and soon the Cycle Exhibition was housed in a colossal 400-foot long marquee, and supported by fifty or so of the leading manufacturers and distributors of cycles, cycle accessories and equipment.

On the occasion of the 25th rally in 1969, Harold Briercliffe, a well known cycling journalist, pointed out that the cycle show attracted greater support from the leading manufacturers than the industry's own annual show, and there were also likely to be more cycle dealers present. Harold also drew attention to the fact that the Yorkshire tourists who put on the rally were just ordinary people, not professional showmen, who annually brought 20,000 people to York and during its twenty-five years nearly half a million.

In those days there was much competition among exhibitors eager to stage the best display. The result was the magnificent displays by such a Bluemels, Carlton, Dawes, Holdsworth, Ron Kitching, Bob Jackson, Middlemores, Raleigh, Jack Taylor, Ed Williams etc., Unfortunately, perhaps due to some extent to the fact that half the exhibition has become something resembling a street market with sales to the public permitted, we now see the infusion of certain ragged displays. Perhaps something can be done to encourage a higher standard of presentation.

Of course, everything was not always plain sailing for the organizers, as for instance, at the very first rally it proved impossible, in those days of food rationing, to obtain the services of a caterer – impossible, that was, until a certain enterprising citizen of York turned up and dispensed cups of tea from an urn which was strapped to his back! Then there was that never-to-be-forgotten occasion when, with one hour to go, word came through that the vehicle bringing the Welsh Bicycle Polo team for our major sports feature had broken down and would not arrive in time. Happily, someone remembered that a team had recently been formed in York, and so after a lightning round up, four local cyclists finished the day representing Wales!

Particular highlights in the history of the rally must be the occasions when the event was officially elevated to international status. The first of these was in 1948 when the Alliance Internationale de Tourisme (AIT) adopted it for their annual cycling rally. On this occasion the already vastly increased crowd was augmented by many hundreds of cyclists from abroad, with most European countries being represented. The committee decided that accommodation should be provided for our visitors, and it was astounding how local cyclists and citizens, often unconnected with

Renee Menzies during the year's mileage record ride (63,000 miles).

cycling, rallied round. Norman and Peggy Bottomley worked like Trojans in fulfilling this task, and many lasting friendships were established. Incidentally this was the occasion of the club's 70th birthday. The AIT joined us again in 1953, the club's 75th anniversary, and in 1965. These were the 'official' International Rallies but many overseas visitors have attended each year. The visitor's book bears the names of hundreds of cyclists, not only from European countries but from the USA, Japan and New Zealand.

The committee has never accepted, nor sought, any form of sponsorship, preferring to be entirely responsible for all aspects of the rally, and no charge is made for admission to the ground nor to the cycle exhibition.

One of the most pleasing features of the rally through the years has been the impeccable behaviour of those participating. Considering the vast numbers involved, this must be regarded as remarkable and has brought favourable comment from the local press, as from the civic authority and the police. Of course the rally resulted in considerable publicity and throughout the years the press, together with the broadcasting and television authorities, have shown a great deal of interest in it, often with considerable coverage. Traditionally the weather has been fine for the event, but inevitably there have been hiccups, with the 1956 rally most likely to linger in the memory of those who participated. Following days of torrential rain we had high hopes that it would have rained itself out by the Friday. But no such luck – the indescribable conditions persisted right across the weekend, while, to add to our concern, the rally had been transferred to a new site – said to be better drained!. Needless to say the attendance was down on the expected twenty thousand but even so about six thousand braved the elements, including a couple of hundred under canvas. The usual York Rally spirit prevailed, however, while so far as I can recollect no event had to be cancelled. To see the competitors in the cycle track events ploughing their way round the arena really was something to marvel at.

In the fifties, with the war not long over, there was not much choice when it came to equipment and the almost universal wet-weather wear was a yellow cape. Consequently, during the field events the arena was surrounded by a broad golden ring of spectators. The trials and tribulations of the participants who finished the day soaked, spattered and bedraggled (but certainly not downhearted) could be understood, but there were others who are not likely to forget the 1956 rally. At the end the exhibitors had to dismantle their stands and load up their vehicles for the journey back to home base. Consequently lorry after lorry, van after van, and car after car became bogged down in the mire. Truly the Knavesmire.

On a happier note let us consider the club's 75th birthday rally. It was once more supported by the AIT, with five hundred cyclists from abroad augmenting the usual rally attendance, while as a special feature the Council decided to re-enact the historic ride in 1878 of the then secretary, Stanley Cotterel, who rode an Ordinary cycle from Edinburgh to Harrogate. Bob Riddell made the arrangements. A.G. Nuttall of the Mid-Yorks DA represented Cotterel and Johnny Mapplebeck of Bradford represented S.H. Ineson, the treasurer. Both wore appropriate costume of green Norfolk jacket and knickerbockers with stiff collar and tie. Riding their Ordinaries they continued their ride to

Peter Rowntree (York Rally President for many years).

the Knavesmire. On the Saturday evening Reg Shaw gave a film show while a dance took place in the Assembly Rooms. Later, round a huge fire, a great international sing-song was held.

On the Knavesmire all the usual events took place, culminating in the Grand Pageant depicting the history of cycling with riders, in appropriate costume, riding bicycles and tricycles from the bone-shaker right up to the modern touring cycle. The whole was augmented by a band playing appropriate music as each group entered the arena. Bob broadcast a suitable commentary. This was possibly the most successful of the whole series of rallies. The police estimate of the attendance over the two days was 30,000.

Needless to say to organize an event of such magnitude has called for considerable effort on the part of those responsible for the conduct of the various rally features. Those principally involved, in one capacity or another, are numerous, but we must give special mention of Peter Rowntree, who from the very start in 1945 did such invaluable work on our behalf. Supported by his wife Eve Rowntree, he was the rally President from the inception until failing health caused him to relinquish the position. Then there is Bob Carmichael-Riddell (CTC Councillor, Leeds). Bob was the original committee chairman, a position he held for very many years; George Bennett (Bradford) chief steward for many years; Norman Bottomley (York) committee chairman; Eric Brearley (Halifax) organiser of the photographic competition and cashier; George Cadman (Harrogate) field events official; Bill Priestley (Leeds), commentator; Peter Danby (Leeds) publicity adviser; Bill Duff (York) cashier; Arnold Elsegood (York) on the field cycle show manager along with Peter Danby; Frank and Jean Gibbs (Hull) sales officers; Ron Healey (York); Chris Jennings (Leeds) equipment officer; Ernie Newman (Sheffield) sales officer; Margaret Carmichael-Riddell (Leeds), catering manageress; Glen Robson (South Shields) events co-ordinator; Peter Wilson (Hull) entries clerk & photographic competition organiser; Brian Witty (Hull), chief camp steward; Trevor Wheatcroft (Hull), chief camp steward; John Wood (York) sales officer; Keith Wray (York) chief steward; and Sam Yaffin (Leeds) for many years the Rally Host. But then, of course, we must not forget the splendid contribution made by our friends from the British Cycling Federation who organized and controlled the cycle grass track events, George Cadman, George Cressell and others. For thirty-four years Ida worked with me and took much of the strain, whilst doing invaluable work in assisting exhibitors in the Cycle Exhibition marquee to establish their stands.

Norman Bottomley was awarded the club's Merit Medallion in 1977. Stanley Cotterel, the first secretary of the CTC when it was founded at Harrogate in 1878, said that he regarded companionship as the foremost attribute of cycle touring, and his club, which in 1950 was able to boast 53,574 members, he described as 'an organization for the formation of friendships on a large scale'. And so it has been with the York Rally, where a great atmosphere has been so apparent. Many friendships have been made and annually renewed at York, an event attracting as many as 20,000 devotees of cycling which has been described by an American visitor as 'the greatest event of its kind in the world'.

7

After the War

By the time we were settling down to something like normal conditions after the war, I found that I had become quite content to enjoy moderate runs which would permit us to take a greater interest in the flora and fauna of the countryside, and at the same time make greater use of the camera. Ida too was quite content with this more leisurely activity, although we still sometimes rode with the club, generally the Easy Riders. This section was designed to provide runs which might be up to a hundred miles or so, but carried out at a comfortable place. The Easy Riders were the originators of the annual 'vets' twelve-hour rides.

Having become involved in organizing the annual York Rally and other activities I am afraid I cannot remember much of the early post-war cycling apart from tours, nor did I keep up my diaries. But I do remember the dreadful winter of 1947 when we were off the road for weeks, having given in to some of the most foul weather in living memory. Eventually we were able to get up to the Wolds by about March (or was it April?) and then found that the main topic of conversation among Woldsfolk was the winter they had experienced. Villages had been cut off for weeks, sheep buried in deep snow drifts, and there had been problems getting food supplies.

One of the Vets twelve-hour rides in the fifties proved to be quite memorable. Tommy Thompson, a greatly respected member and one, perhaps, more entitled to be termed a 'Vet' than most of us, had been south to take part in a twelve-hour event based on the London area, and while there had persuaded about half a dozen or so of the riders to come up to Yorkshire and take part in our event.

Our members rallied round, and we were able to provide accommodation for our guests. They proved to be splendid people and we all enjoyed the change of company. One of them was a vegetarian, and he was given into the care of Bunny Stephenson who was put into a rare state of panic, not knowing what a vegetarian fed on! Then there was a very elegant gentleman who turned out to be the local bank manager from somewhere in darkest Buckinghamshire, whilst one was a Cockney postman who was domiciled with Ida and me. I am sure they all enjoyed their visit as much as we did.

Cycle–Rail Excursions

In 1949 the club had negotiated with British Railways for the provision of special vans for the carriage of cycles. These vans, first used on the boat trains of the Southern Region, were in regular use between London and the Channel ports, but eventually, by 1957, cycle-rail excursions were being arranged. Of course, the Hull and East Riding DA wasn't going to be left out and I organized an excursion from Hull to Windermere. Special vans were used, each fitted with hooks to suspend the cycles by the front wheel; each could carry eighty-six cycles. The Hull Thursday Road Club, and the Ramblers Association joined us, whilst a mid-Yorkshire contingent were picked up in Bradford. Thus a full train-load arrived in Windermere, where they split up into parties and went in their various ways. Bill Oakley, Chairman of the Club Council and Reg Shaw, National Secretary, met us at Windermere, arriving there from Blackpool, where they had been attending a meeting of the Club Council on the Saturday, as indeed had I. But in my case I had had to dash back home so that I could see the cycle-rail excursion launched on the Sunday morning. The event was voted a great success but it proved to be a one and only as when we endeavoured to organize a second excursion, British Railways set a minimum number of passengers and, if memory serves me correctly, an increased fare, to which we could not agree.

But the idea of assisted transport to enable us to get further afield appealed so we switched to a small bus, suitably fitted up to carry a dozen or so cycles. Thus equipped we had successful outings to Derbyshire, one to Pickering and another to Rosedale. On the occasions of the Derbyshire and Pickering outings we met, by arrangement, a contingent from the Sheffield DA.

It is a well known fact that we do not get as much snow these days as in years gone by. Nevertheless, it was not usual to get snow at Easter but one never-to-be-forgotten year (I suppose it was in the early fifties) we really got a snorter. Several parties of local cyclists, taking advantage of the long weekend, were away touring in the Dales, Derbyshire, the Lakes etc., and while the weather was nothing to write home about at the start it steadily deteriorated and by the Monday heavy snow arrived as the parties headed for home. The conditions worsened to the extent that the prospect of reaching Hull at all became questionable, so when they arrived at York the CTC party made a most unusual decision – they would take the train to Hull (those were the days when the York

Ida on Ben Nevis.

to Hull line still operated). The journey proceeded without incident as far as Market Weighton where a party of Hull Thursday RC members, having thrown in the towel, decided that they too would complete the journey to Hull by train – trusting that they would not be observed doing the unthinkable. Imagine, then, their horror when they discovered the CTC party already aboard. That took a lot of living down.

Some Post-War Tours

Our first foreign tour after the war was when we joined Reg Shaw for a tour of the Ardennes in 1947. I cannot remember much of the tour, nor of those in the party, except that Ted Bannister of the headquarters staff was with us, also Rita and Ernest Scott of the Nottingham DA; Ernest was then their secretary. Rita's father had a manufacturing business with premises in Nottingham but he also had business connections in Belgium, which he frequently had occasion to visit. At the time there were restrictions on the amount of money which could be taken abroad, so we cycle tourists, with modest cash requirements, arranged to take the maximum and pass over the surplus to Rita's father.

The main object of our visit to the Ardennes was to attend the AIT rally in Furfuz, the first AIT international rally after the war. I hoped that I would learn something about rally organizing from the visit, but as it turned out, the event was run on entirely different lines to our York Rally, and as the attendance could not have been more than a hundred or so, with everything of such an informal nature, the event was, from our point of view, rather a dead loss!

However, we did meet some interesting cyclists and one I well remember was Dr Wattyn, who attracted attention with his cycle which incorporated two of his own inventions. Firstly he had a two-position saddle, operated by a lever below the saddle, by means of which it could be moved upward and forward while ascending a hill. This, he alleged, increased efficiency. At the same time, his second invention came into use. This involved a rocking action to the handlebars which transmitted an auxiliary powering action to the transmission. I never heard that either of these ideas ever got on the market.

Of course, the war had only recently concluded and there was considerable evidence of war damage, and even abandoned tanks. What impressed me was that the Belgians had immediately commenced reconstruction. We saw a bank which had been severely damaged and which was in the process of being reconstructed. While work was still in progress the parts of the building that had been completed were already in use.

But, of course, this was a cycling tour and we thoroughly explored the Ardennes and the adjacent area.

We visited Corsica in 1932 with Olive and Ernie Newman of Sheffield. Ernie, incidentally, was the cashier and hard working sales chief in the York Rally cause! The tour proved to be one of the best ever and Corsica a superb cycling country with virtually no traffic outside the towns.

Madge and Eddie Rayner were with us for our Norwegian tour in 1964, when I was interested to see how the roads compared with those of my last visit in 1932. Well, they proved to be pretty much the same and while the scenery was obviously, unchanged, the almost incessant rain was in direct contrast to the earlier conditions.

Then there was south-west Ireland in 1967, just Ida and me this time, and how we enjoyed this wonderful corner of the world: Cork, Kerry and the Dingle peninsula. The countryside was beautiful and the people delightfully friendly and amusing.

In was in 1955 that we joined Les Warner for a tour of the celebrated Gorges of the Tarn in southern France. Most of the party were Les's friends from the London area but they made a splendid party and with perfect weather and some memorable scenery it went down well.

The Scottish Highlands

Of course, interspersed with the continental tours were various tours in the Scottish Highlands. I think I have accounted for fifteen or so tours in the Highlands through the years and this must remain our favoured touring ground.

In the early years we would have ridden through the night on the first day to ensure a flying start, then it would be Edinburgh or Glasgow for the first night's stop. Later we would take the train to Fort William or Inverness while heading for the north-west which I suppose was our favourite area. We used to say that the best of the Highlands was beyond the Caledonian Canal although there are other choice bits such as Braemar,

On the Torridon footpath.

Balmoral, Tomintoul area, the Ardnamurchan peninsula, and of course the islands of Mull and Skye.

Perhaps our favourite was the Torridon area – we went back there time after time after time. How we enjoyed the Shieldaig to Torridon ride involving the exquisite 'Torridon Footpath'. This led by a rough road through Balgy, then into the beautiful woods, with rhododendrons, a marvellous display of ferns, and a moss covered terrain, with all the time Upper Loch Torridon and those delightful mountains Ben Alligin, Liachach and Ben Eighe keeping us company. Sometimes we would reach Shieldaig by way of Applecross, having crossed over the Beallach Pass from Tornapress on Loch Kishorn, thence that delightful bridle path which overlooked Applecross Bay for a full twenty miles.

Now, unhappily, both the footpath and the coast road have been

Loch Torridon.

obliterated by modern roads. I suppose we must not be selfish and perhaps the new roads will enable some people to see this marvellous area who would not otherwise do so . But what a tragedy – the Torridon Footpath, gone for ever!

The ferry crossings were a very important and enjoyable part of the Highland tour. We always looked forward to them and considered any delays there might be a necessary part of the tour. I think we must have used most of them, some on many occasions. Those which come to mind particularly are Ballachulish on Loch Leven, and Corron across the narrows on Loch Linnhe, where at one time I remember the method of calling the ferryman across from the other side was by sounding a gong. There was Kyle (for the Isle of Skye) and Strome – here the calling up system was by means of a bugle which was attached to a pole. There was Lochaline, the crossing to Salen on Mull and Kylesku which I recall was a free ferry at a time when the County Council were endeavouring to attract more tourists to the area! But I am leaving the two most important to the last. The Cape Wrath ferry operated between Keodale and the far side (the ferryman's house). This was a rowing boat crossing and a prelude to what some years earlier was a hectic journey on a rough and stony road with broken bridges terminating at the lighthouse. Now, of course there is a decent road to the lighthouse. Lastly, we had the

At the Strome Ferry – calling the ferryman.

Ullapool to Altnaharrie ferry, again a journey by rowing boat. Many years ago, when the ferryman lived in Ullapool, it is said that if you landed up on the Cape Wrath side the procedure for attracting the attention of the ferryman, a mile or so away, was to light a fire on the shore of the Kyle!

They tell me that already three of the ferries have been replaced by bridges: Ballachulish, Strome and Kylesku, while that at Kyle is in the offing, but it will be a long time before they get around to bridging Loch Broom between Ullapool and Altnaharrie!

Landing on the Island of Gruinard was forbidden during the war – in fact the ban existed until quite recently – because certain experiments with anthrax were conducted there.

I could go on for long enough about the glorious Highlands, but before I get completely carried away, I will just mention three Scottish incidents. One very wet day soon after the war, Ida and I decided to call it a day when we reached Aultbea on Loch Awe and booked in at the Autlbea Hotel, where after a clean up we had afternoon tea in the lounge. A lady and gentleman, the only other guests, made room for us nearer the fire (it was that sort of day), when the lady noticed that Ida's

C.P. and Ida on the Applecross bridle path.

coat was slightly damp (it was nothing more than a bit of condensation) and insisted on taking her up to her room. There Ida was decked out in a very sophisticated garment – much to her delight! It was then that the gentleman decided that something should be done about me and I was carted away to emerge in a senior naval officer's coat. Talk about laugh! It turned out that Loch Awe had been used as a base for supply ships operating between the British Isles and the USA and he was in charge of the base which was in the process of being closed down. It turned out that, coming from Grimsby, he knew Ida's uncle, a Humber pilot based in Grimsby! Small world, isn't it?

Then there was the occasion when, having stayed the night in Braemar at the CTC house, we made our way as far as Balmoral before turning away northward on our way to Tomintoul. There we came upon a large marquee from which issued, at that very moment, the whole of the Royal party. Presumably, having had lunch, they were returning to the moors

Loch Maree – Ken Hughes.

to continue their shooting! It was interesting to see their method of regaining the top of the moor. A Land Rover (or similar vehicle) trailed a long rope behind to which clung members of the party to make easier their ascent of the moor. They were all there except Prince Philip who, disdaining the rope, went off on his own and, having allowed me to pass by, crossed the road and ascended the moor unaided.

And now for incident number three. After leaving the far north- west, Frank, Ken and I were heading southward having left Tongue and were making for Liarg. On passing a farmhouse which was about two or three hundred yards off the road, we became aware of three sheep dogs which rushed out from the farmhouse and made straight for us. They separated, one taking the direct course, one heading somewhat behind us, presumably to cut off any possible retreat, while the third was making to get ahead of us. Well, notable coward that I am, and realising that an encounter was imminent, I decided that discretion was the best part of valour and went flat out to get ahead of dog number three. Fear lent speed to my endeavours and I got ahead of the dog which then gave up the chase to join the rounding up party. Feeling safe, I stopped and enjoyed the fun of seeing Frank and Ken rounded up like sheep at the roadside. Fortunately for them, someone at the farm saw what was going on and called the dogs off.

Breakdowns and Repairs

I suppose we never had a lot to complain about regarding breakages, tyre troubles and so forth, so perhaps things are not so much different today compared with former years. Being a cautious type I have always carried a spare inner tube, but I recently heard of a young lady, a new member, who had recently suffered an incurable tyre problem and so now carries not only a spare tube, but a spare lightweight, flexible-edged racing tyre – just as a spare. How's that for caution? As for me, I once had a peculiar mishap. I was riding immediately behind Harry Suddaby at the time, near North Grimston, and having got ahead of the club, was riding slowly, at the same time looking over my shoulder to see if they were coming. Unknown to me, Harry had stopped. Now, Harry's cycle at the time was fitted with hub wingnuts of a particularly savage type and as I smacked into him my front tyre was slashed to ribbons. The tube was no problem, but the tyre? We got round the problem on that occasion by binding the tyre and rim together with wire, then pumping up in the normal way. It put the brake out of commission, of course, but it got me home.

The only times I had real trouble were both in the early thirties, before I got a decent '531' framed cycle. I was riding on the ridge road, somewhere south of Caister in Lincolnshire, when my front forks decided they had had enough and both blades broke off just below the crown. That really had me whacked, so there was nothing else for it but to start walking. Luckily I caught a bus to New Holland at Caister, and the ferry got me back to Hull.

What about the other time? Well, again on that same cycle, the top tube snapped and once more I was reduced to catching a bus.

I have heard of various antidotes to serious tyre trouble. In my case I used wire, but I have heard of a badly split cover being stitched with thread, the thread being brought round the wire edging of the cover and producing a respectable repair. Then, of course, there is the time-honoured stuffing of the tyre with grass, though I never came across anyone with first-hand knowledge of this form of first aid!

I don't know whether this comes into the category of tyre trouble ingenuity, but early in the war I sustained a puncture (they really didn't occur that often), while on the York road somewhere near Market Weighton.

Before I tackled the repair one of those great big vehicles with a 6oft. trailer pulled up. The driver was taking a Spitfire, in a whacking big crate, to King George Dock in Hull, and whereas he had been given a route to follow what had been overlooked was the height of the crate. Could we tell him how to get there without having to pass under any bridges?

So I suggested that if he would take me and my cycle on board and deliver me at home, I would see him safely through. Thus I was saved the trouble of mending the puncture! And didn't the neighbours stare when I arrived home on an Aircraft Carrier!

How the DA copes with the Present

How has the DA fared since the war? Well, on the whole, I should think pretty satisfactorily. But we must not try and relate present day achievements with those of earlier times, as with increased wealth has come the availability of other forms of activity, while television must have had a retrograde effect on attendance at club events, particularly at the clubroom. But perhaps the motor car has proved to be the biggest enemy. Happily, in recent years there has arisen an increasing concern about health and, quite rightly, many people are turning to physical activities of one form or another. This is where cycling can benefit.

Annual dinner at Beverley (1945).

Some older members at Lissett (1946). Top row: C.P., Bill Adams, Jack Bailey,
Charlie Nicholson, Harry Wharton, Harry Johnson, 'Gill' Gilleard, and Bill
Okey. Front: Frank Suddaby, Mrs Adams, Mrs Bailey, Lilian Nicholson,
Marie Gilleard and George Reeder.

The DA has, through the years, always provided runs for members through a variety of sections, catering for varying requirements. The names of these sections were intended to indicate the style of ride provided, such as Social, Easy Riders, Rendezvous, General, Intermediate, Loiterers, Family, Hardriders, Century, while today I see that an effort has been made to simplify the position by just calling them A, B, C etc. – though I fail to see how this can indicate the type of ride provided.

The family section was brought into being following the war with Harry Suddaby at the helm, and quickly became most popular. The youngsters were conveyed in a variety of ways. Depending on age, this was often in sidecars or trailers drawn by either solo or tandem. For the older children, a device known as 'kiddie cranks' was available. Attached in the position for the rear rider of a tandem, this consisted of a mini-chainset with shorter cranks and carried at a suitable height for the shorter legs of the rider. By chain the device was connected to the transmission of the tandem.

Club runs are today being well supported, with turnouts sometimes topping fifty, while standard rides are as popular as ever. A pleasing point about runs support today is that several prominent members of local racing clubs are now, after more or less retiring from racing, finding our club runs suit them down to the ground.

Typical amongst these is Arthur Anderson (formerly Honorary Secretary, Hull Clarion), Ron and Betty Philipson and Vic Sutton. Vic Sutton was formerly a member of the Thorne Paragon Club and is known nationally, and even internationally, with brilliant performances on the sporting side of cycling. He is one of the few riders in this country who have competed in the Tour de France and other principal Continental events, more than once finishing amongst the leaders.

Others who, in recent years, have done much to keep the Hull DA flag flying include Helen Cockerell, Brian Crossland, Frank and Janice Martinson, John Osgerby, Paul Grannon, Bob Pank, Ann and Brian Railton, Jim and Sheila Sampson, Simon Smith, Maurice Tomlinson and Don Wilkinson.

Many will have been interested in the exploits of Paul Claxton, whose young life ended so tragically while on a mountaineering expedition in Indonesia while acting as official photographer with Operation Raleigh, Paul did much of his cycling as a member of the Hull DA. In 1987 he delivered the Saturday evening slide show at the York Rally based on his Alaskan adventure. Apart from Alaska, he toured extensively in Morocco, the Sahara Desert and many parts of Europe.

The DAs are a great source of recruitment for the club – in fact, I think it is fair to say, the principal one. For myself I suppose over the years I must have enrolled a fair number of new members, but I have never kept a record. However, Bill Oakley, in his book *Winged Wheel*, mentioned that in 1955 I was responsible for thirty-nine new members, so I suppose that the total over the years must have been pretty impressive.

It may not be generally known that the DA once won an award: The Carter Ruck Trophy. This was in 1957 and the award was for the DA attaining the greatest percentage increase of new members in the year. This was the first year of the presentation, when the DA made the astonishing increase of 25%.

The clubroom does not get the regular hundred per cent attendances of pre-war days, but with so many counter-attractions this is not surprising. It seems to be a problem many organizations are faced with. Travel talks and slide shows are the most popular clubroom events, just as they always were, and the DA owes a lot to Pete Wilson who does a fine job organizing and presenting these shows. Pete came on the scene directly after the war, and has been a tower of strength ever since. Apart from his work as Social Secretary, Pete has, on numerous occasions, entertained us with his beautifully presented slide shows, mostly depicting his, and his wife Maria's, cycling activities. Pete is renowned through the country.

The DA War Memorial

This was established in memory of those members who lost their lives during the 1939 – 1945 war and took the form of a bronze plate, suitably engraved and incorporating a clock. This was originally established at the DA headquarters at 84a Spring Bank. The member deemed to have rendered the greatest service to the DA during the year was awarded a smaller plaque and the names of the recipients were added annually.

1949	R.C. Witty	1959	A. F. Galleard
1950	C.W. Newmarch	1960	A. Campbell
1951	A. Benson	1961	F. G. Gibbs
1952	G.E. Munson	1961	W. Bunting A. Newby
1953	B. Outhwaite	1963	M. Dixie Mrs J. Gibbs
1954	Miss E.M. Brumhead	1964	H. Suddaby
1955	C.H. Waudby	1965	Mrs I. Pratt
1956	A. Campbell	1966	B. Fairweather
1957	H. Alexander	1967	Mr & Mrs G. R. Philipson
1958	C.A. Pratt	1968	R. A. Whitfield

1969	R. J. Jennison	1981	A. F. Gilleard
1970	S. Watkinson	1982	R. A. Whitfield
1971	B. Witty	1983	T. Wilkinson
1972	B. Fairweather.	1984	K. Dalton
1973	R. A. Whitfield	1985	T. Wilkinson
1974	A. Newby	1986	Mr & Mrs H. Suddaby
1975	Mrs J. Gibbs	1987	T. Wheatcroft
1976	T. Wheatcroft	1988	T. Wheatcroft
1977	A. P. Wilson	1989	T. Wilkinson
1978	M. Tomlinson	1990	P. L. Dove
1979	Mrs D. Wheatcroft	1991	D. Teale
1980	T. O'Connor		

Office Bearers and Other Prominent Members

Who were the principal officers throughout the years? Well, the first President was Lt. Commander Kenworthy MP (we aimed high in those days!) and he was followed by E. Parker Walker in 1933, who in turn gave way to Cliff Pratt in 1950. Then came A.F. 'Gill' Gilleard in 1967 leading on to the current President, Alan Newby, in 1987. Incidentally, Alan's brother, Les, was a member of the Clarion Bicycle Polo team with whom we had many a memorable battle!

The original Secretary in 1925 was C.H. Fry, replaced by Eddie Bacon in 1927, followed by Bob Craggy in 1928 and Cliff Pratt in 1934 – until 1951. Things got a bit hazy after that, but I believe Cyril Newmarch came next, before Paddy Meenagh took over, and then Harold Alexander, Ben Fairweather, Ron Whitfield, Trevor Wilkinson, Pete Dove, Ann Railton and now again Pete Dove.

For Treasurer, first we had A.F. Gilleard for a considerable number of years before Bernard Outhwaite took over, and now we have Dennis Teal. The current Committee Chairman is Eric Brumhead. The present membership stands at 356. The official DA colours, as decided in 1925, are purple and amber!

Pre-war, Harry Wharton did a greatly appreciated job in producing a monthly magazine, *Herda*, which was, of course, replaced by the *Forces News Letter* during the way. At the end of the fifties, Frank Gibbs, and Jean produced an excellent quarterly, the *Woldsman*, which was continued for twenty years. Now Jim Sampson has stepped in and is producing a resurrected quarterly under the same title.

Of others having a good deal to do with the success of the DA is

Invitation veterans' 12-hour ride (1955).

Brian Witty. Shortly after the war, Brian worked on various farms, first of all in the East Riding, and eventually on a farm in Nidderdale where, amongst other crafts, he learnt the art of dry stone walling! Later, he spent many hours on voluntary work, particularly with the Youth Hostels Association, which work often included his speciality, wall building. Two projects which come to mind are the Wheeldale Youth Hostel and, more recently, the reconstruction of the Beverley Friary, again for the YHA.

Apart from being members of the CTC and YHA, Brian and his wife Pauline are closely associated with other organisations concerned with the countryside, such as the Council for the Preservation of Rural England. It is not surprising that, in view of his readiness to help others, he is a member of the Beech Holme Tandem Section, which, of course, provides cycling facilities for blind members, whilst he has been known

C.P. receives the AIT Gold Medal from Reg Shaw (President of the AIT Cycle Touring Committee).

to devote a couple of days in the middle of a cycling tour to repairing a wall for some farmer!

It seems incredible that it is about twenty years since we lost Gus Campbell. For thirty years he was a popular and fantastic worker in a wide variety of capacities for the DA. As Social Secretary, his dogged persistence ensure that there were no blanks in the season's programme. But his work with the club did not rest solely with the social side, as he did a wonderful job in recruiting and leading runs for the youngsters. His work also for the Beech Holme Tandem Section was greatly appreciated. Prior to each run of the tandem club, Gus would 'phone or call on all members to get an assurance of their attendance!

Marie Gilleard was one of the original Hardriders. She earned fame in 1971 when, at the age of seventy-one, she successfully completed the club's National Veterans' Triennial 100 mile ride, being then the oldest woman to do so.

Harry Flynn has been prominent in Beverley affairs for a considerable number of years, mainly as a Councillor, while he has served as Mayor of the Borough several times. Harry rode with us in the thirties and well remembers some of those wonderful occasions, but he is still an active cyclist. In more recent years he has become well known for his work for charity. On no fewer than seventeen occasions he has delivered much needed supplies to Poland.

Awards Gained by DA Members

Honorary life membership CTC (National):   C.A. Pratt (1949)
The Sir Alfred Bird Memorial Prize (National): C.A. Pratt (1945)
Certificate of Merit (UK):   E. C. Sanderson (Scarborough) (1937)
                               A. F. Gilleard (1950)
                               H. & E. Alexander (1963)
                               A. Campbell (1969)
                               H. Suddaby (1989)
AIT Gold Medal (International):   C. A. Pratt (1963)
C. A. Rhodes Memorial Award (Yorkshire Cycling Federation):
                               C. A. Pratt (1964)

The Road Safety Council

For many years, before, during and after the war I was pleased to represent the CTC on the Hull Road Safety Council. Chaired by the Chief Constable, and including the City Engineer and other City officials and

Councillors, all aspects of road usage and (mis-usage) were considered and recommendations made. I was able to put the cyclists' point of view on many road safety topics, in addition to pointing out the numerous indiscretions of other road users. I think I was able to keep the cyclists' end up!

Mountain Bikes and Crash Hats

The safety cycle arrived in 1885, and tolled the knell of the ordinary (penny-farthing) by providing gearing by means of a rear sprocket fitted to the rear hub and connected by a chain to a front chainwheel attached, in turn, to what is now known as the bottom bracket, thus dispensing with the necessity for the enormous front wheel of the ordinary. Since then, this system has reigned supreme though many attempts have been made to improve on it. True, certain modifications have been made such as improved gearing, better brakes, pneumatic tyres and so on. (The original safety was shod with solid tyres.) Of course, there has become available better materials.

Now, however, has come along what was hailed as a real revolution in design in the shape of the mountain bike, though when you come to consider it the basic design is still as J.K. Stanley first established it. I believe the original idea was to provide a cycle for off-road events and to that end the cycle has strengthened wheels fitted with large section tyres resembling those fitted to motor cycles(!). In addition multi-gearing is provided but no mudguards. Even so, our cyclo-cross boys perform wonders on similar terrain but on more orthodox cycles – as indeed, do we humble tourists who do part of our riding on rough bridle paths, etc. I suppose it was inevitable that the manufacturers would produce an inferior version even in children's sizes. Though selling at a horrific price they appear to have made an immediate appeal to the youngsters who are taking to them in tens of thousands – while the craze lasts! The silly thing is that they are used as road machines, a purpose for which they were never intended.

Of course this has been great for the trade and industry, as has been the arrival of the crash hat. If cyclists or, in the case of the youngsters, their parents, feel that they are safer wearing one – well, that's fine, so long as there is never any suggestion that they become compulsory wear. In this respect I would just like to say that in my sixty-six years as a cyclist during which I have ridden 400,000 miles, and through my connection with the cycle trade and as a local and national official bringing me in contact with tens of thousands of cyclists, I have never once heard of a cyclist receiving serious head injuries as a result of a cycling accident.

Photography and Other Activities

Perhaps it was inevitable, being the son of a photographer, that I, too, would become interested in photography, although this did not seem to apply to my three brothers. My first camera at the age, I suppose, of about eight, was a pinhole camera made by my father. This consisted of a light tight box about 4″ high and 3″ wide with a depth of about 3″. The back was removable and provision made for the holding of the emulsion-coated glass plate, whilst on the front, enclosing the lens (pin hole) was glued a small pill box complete with push-on lid which was removed to effect the exposure. This was established by experiment! Cost: nil! This primitive device produced surprisingly good results.

I had, over the years, a whole succession of cameras, the first being a VPK (Vest Pocket Kodak); then I went on to more sophisticated cameras, including a 3¼″ × 3¼″ Zeiss which became my favourite for a number of years. This was the camera that I used for most of my early photography, although somewhere in the thirties I moved to a Rollie – a splendid camera, but what a rotten shape for a cyclist to lug around! Producing 2¼″ square picture, it was a twin lens reflex which accounted for the odd shape.

Of course, I did all my own processing, and when it came to lantern slides, of which I turned out many hundreds, the negative had to be projected through an enlarger on to an emulsion-coated glass plate – in my case 3¼″ × 3¼″. This, when bound up with a cover glass of the same size, was the lantern slide!

In the mid-thirties I experimented with the Dufay colour process which produced good colour though requiring a powerful illumination when screened. Then with the arrival of the Kodak colour film after the war the entire scene was transformed – even though the speed was a mere 8 ASA. At that stage I used a Silette before being bitten by the sound ciné bug in the early sixties. Cycling, walking, cycle frame building etc., provided suitable subjects. My first ciné camera was a Bolex – a Japanese Nisa however took its place before I switched back to still photography – less time-consuming. My cameras at this time were a Practika followed by a Pentax. By then I was deriving great pleasure by producing colour enlargements, blowing up my little transparencies to as large as 12″ × 16″.

I can't recall many cyclists who were gardeners, but my interest in gardening went back even further than in photography. As a youngster, I had been fascinated by plants, but soon tired of watching plants grow – I wanted to grow my own!

Eventually, I got the hang of it all and as the years went by, grew a vast variety of plants, as often as not from seed. Never interested in growing vegetables, my range took in all manner of annuals and perennial and went on to conifers and bonsai. I accumulated a whole forest of miniature trees at one time. Then, as time went on, I acquired a greenhouse and later a conservatory, which opened up an entirely new area of possibilities as, with the addition of heating and propagation equipment, there seemed to be no limits.

It was a real red letter day when we found a 3 ft. grass snake in the pond! Sadly the three hedgehogs which visited our ponds failed to survive their immersion, although I always thought that they could swim. Cold water fish in the garden led to tropicals indoors. But annually in the garden we derived great pleasure from watching the blue tits which nested in the boxes on the side of the shed. Until the day we found one of the parents lying dead nearby. It was not a cat this time: what had happened was that the bird had flown into the door of the conservatory which was in their direct flight path. Well, after studying his mate for some time and looking really sorry for himself, the survivor seemed to come to a decision and forthwith took over the enormous task of providing food for the brood, a task normally undertaken by the two of them. Happily, his valiant efforts proved successful as all were safely launched.

Another incident also concerned blue tits although, unfortunately, this involved tragedy. Hearing a buzzing noise coming from the tit box, I found on investigation that bumble bees had built a nest on top of the tits' nest. Inside were the remains of a full brood of youngsters, all neatly sealed in by the bees. Whether the bees found the nest already abandoned, or whether they killed the youngsters before building their own nest, we will never know.

Pete Wilson got me interested in butterflies and moths, and I found this hobby quite fascinating, and again it provided camera subjects. I used to buy the eggs or pupae from the specialists and simply grow them on until the beautiful adults finally emerged. After providing the correct food plant (some butterflies and moths would rather die than partake of other than their normal food!) and the right temperature, the procedure didn't seem to offer much of a problem. I produced some magnificent specimens of tropical insects which, after they had emerged and been photographed in the conservatory, I used to release outside! I suppose the residents of Cottingham must have thought they were being invaded when huge Giant Atlas Moths, with a wing span of six inches, zoomed by!

In Recent Years

By 1978, although only seventy, I didn't think that I could any longer cope with the traditional club run and my cycling had deteriorated to occasional runs of about twenty-five miles, Ida was no longer able to achieve anything beyond the bare minimum, although we still did a certain amount of walking, usually in Scotland or the Lakes with either Dave or Pete and their respective families. I must say that I was pretty unhappy about things as I had not contemplated becoming old so soon! So when Harry Suddaby said, 'Why don't you join me on weekly runs, sometimes with train assistance on the Scarborough line which will enable us to get to areas that are out of the question otherwise,' I made an instant decision! I was back! Ida was in full agreement. In fact she encouraged me.

Pete Wilson.

Our rides were a great success and we really polished up our knowledge of the Wolds with runs of forty miles or so, or up to fifty miles which was about the limit. After sixty years we were still able to find stretches of road which were new to us. Later, on his retirement, we were joined by Eddie Rayner, an old colleague from the Hardriding days – but now severely toned down! Then later still, Ernie Drewery made it a quartet, again on

Frank and Jean Gibbs with Harry and Frances Suddaby.

retirement. Ernie was best known in the days of Bob Craggy, Tom Garniss, etc., whilst both of them rode with the family section in the fifties.

I have one particular recollection of this period. During a pause in our run one day, and not ten miles from York, we halted by a bridge and were watching the activities of a water vole, when we were thrilled to see a kingfisher streak along the stream with a brilliant flash of blue, before vanishing round a bend. It really made our day.

I had a bit of an interruption in 1979 when, possibly due to the stress of the York Rally and Ida's illness, I had a stroke. It wasn't too bad but left me with a co-ordination problem. I couldn't type for some time. (Why, when I struck G, did it say T?). But I got back on the bike and had more wonderful rides until 1984 when, with Ida not improving, I had another stroke. Though I was in hospital for eight days and now had a balance problem, it wasn't too bad. Then Ida died in 1985. I had a memorial seat established on the village green at Lund – one of her favourite villages.

Using the trains so frequently, we got to know the guards quite well, and were getting along famously until the day a new guard appeared and did the inexcusable. He refused to allow our cycles on the train, despite there being plenty of room in the guards' van. We were furious and had words with the regional officials – with some success. I don't know what went on behind the scenes, but that guard became as helpful and friendly as can be. Sometime later, Harry, on being refused putting his tandem on a train at Peterborough, had all his trouble straightened out when our old enemy-cum-friend appeared on the scene (having been transferred down south) and, recognising Harry, allowed him to take his tandem on a non-cycle-carrying train! His parting shot was, 'Don't forget to tell Cliff Pratt!' So good did come out of evil!

Then came the sad day of the arrival of the Sprinter trains, when we learned that there would be no room for our cycles. A blow indeed, as it was for numerous other cyclists, many of whom relied on trains for connecting with journeys to and from work. It looked as if we were going to be restricted to the area within a day's ride. So David made us a trailer capable of carrying the cycles and with the aid of Eddie's car, we were once more able to get further afield. In fact it opened up an entirely new territory.

Then we lost Harry's company, although he and Frances are still able to enjoy limited riding on the tandem. Incidentally, when I joined the club in 1927, Harry was already a well established member, having joined earlier. He had even gained a place on the committee, which was pretty exceptional in those days for a comparatively new member!

A couple of years ago Harry achieved fame when the BBC included him in a feature about cycling. Representing the older fraternity, he and Frances were filmed in a variety of locations – riding, of course their tandem.

Hull Street Life Museum of Transport

Steve Goodhand, Keeper of Transport, the leading light in the establishment of the new transport museum, persuaded me to part with much material for the project. My 'pride and joy', an old cast-iron CTC Repairers sign now graces the front of a mock up 1930s cycle shop, while numerous photographs, press cuttings, plaques, badges etc. were all found room in the impressive display. Then there are three of my films: *Alan's Bike* concerns the construction of a cycle frame, *Cycle Cross* an event staged by the Humber Velo Club and *The York Rally*. These, transferred on to videotape, are on permanent showing. 1930s cycle touring is depicted in two of my pre-war slide shows – *The Firs and Fjords of Norway*

Three old 'uns.

and *Bosnia*, now war-torn. The slides are automatically projected along with commentary. The DA's pre-war projector is also on display.

And So On

I wonder what has become of all our colleagues of the thirties? Inevitably, some are no longer with us though Harry Suddaby and Eddie Rayner are still to some extent active. In Eddie's case not only does he ride with us on Wednesdays but he also walks with the CHA, to saying nothing of swimming and goodness knows what else! Geo. Munson is another who has deserted to the walkers (is walking an easier option?). I had a word with Reg 'Skid' Colman recently who is, unfortunately, now a resident in the Rockcliffe Home for the Blind. But what about K.C. 'Casey' Redfearn, Cyril Garner and Eric Charles?

I have had a wonderful cycling life, so far, having explored extensively the Yorkshire Wolds, the Moors and the Dales and to a slightly lesser degree the Lakes, Scotland and the Derbyshire Peak district, to say nothing of other parts of the British Isles. I have enjoyed fantastic tours in Norway,

Yugoslavia, Corsica, Ireland (North and South), Bavaria and the Austrian, Swiss and Italian Alps. On many of these tours I was accompanied by my wife, Ida, and what memories are conjured up! So now, with the hills getting steeper, and the miles longer, Eddie, Ernie and I still head for the Wolds on Wednesdays and, taking advantage of the by-ways and bridleways, continue to enjoy the delights and freedom cycling provides.

8

The Incredible Dolomites

It was in August 1936 that six of us, all members of the Cyclists' Touring Club, left Hull on the SS *Melrose Abbey*, bound for Rotterdam, on the first stage of a journey which was to take us through Bavaria, Austria and the Italian Dolomites.

Leaving the steamer on arriving in Rotterdam, we had to cross the city to the Maas station, where we 'tucked in' behind a cycling policeman who, finding us more or less lost, kindly led us through the complications of the city. And did he make us ride! He took us over awkward bridges, round acute corners on greasy stone sets, and across tramlines at such a speed that we had difficulty in keeping him in sight.

After an uneventful, all-night journey across Germany we arrived in Munich at 7 a.m. and we immediately headed for a restaurant, where an excellent breakfast put us in good shape for our first spell of cycling.

The party was made up of Fred Greenway, Ken Hughes, Bernard Outhwaite, Dan Rowe and myself, all of the Hull area, together with John Smithson who hailed from the West Riding.

We thought that we had left all possibility of rain behind when we left England, but it wasn't so and rain was falling when we retrieved our cycles and set off along the Rosenheimer Strasse, one of the main roads out of Munich, and headed for the Austrian border.

We soon came to the start of one of Germany's famous Autobahns, roads reserved for the use of fast motor traffic only, for which, for the privilege of using, a toll was charged. No motorist appeared to be using it, however, all preferring to use the ordinary road, along which they tore at a most unseemly speed!

The road was cobbled, so we used the cycle paths provided. These were narrow and necessitated riding in single file, while periodically we had to dodge trees and so on. Still, it was better than the road.

The early rain soon ceased and the clouds were showing distinct signs of breaking by the time we had covered a few miles, when we were riding on a broad, good surfaced road across gently undulating country, while away to the south was visible the outline of the Bavarian Alps, conveying the promise of things to come. The villages we passed through were typically Bavarian, consisting of colour-washed cottages adorned with window boxes of attractive flowers and trailing vines. The people were dressed invariably in the well known Bavarian costume, the men wearing leather shorts and white stockings, a short grey flannel jacket, with green collar and cuffs, and those little felt hats, complete with feather. Picturesque oxen carts were common, and to us a source of great interest.

By this time we were getting along in fine style, the weather, the scenery and our spirits improving with every turn of the pedals. At Bad Aibling, we spent time exploring its interesting streets. Everywhere was displayed the Fascists' red flags bearing the emblem of the swastika. Nearly every building in Bavaria seemed to sport this decoration, varying in size between those outside the large hotels which hung perhaps twenty feet, to the tiny ones fluttering from cottage windows. Much of this decoration was on account of the Olympic Games in progress in Berlin.

A further eight miles brought us to Rosenheim, and here we lunched.

It is interesting that at Munich we were already 1,705 feet above sea level, and the road then rose slightly to 2,000 feet. By now the sun was blazing down and fleecy white clouds chased across the sky. Passing

through the tiny village of Prutting, we noticed a good example of the continental method of hay-making. Owing to the heavy dews, it was necessary to keep the grass off the ground, consequently posts were erected and the grass hung on them to dry.

We were now only a few miles from Berchtesgaden, the home of Adolf Hitler. We found it rather comical that half the men-folk hereabouts had their faces adorned with the Führer's well-known little moustache and forelock, so that to us, it appeared that there were Hitlers everywhere.

Later we came upon the large Chiem See (or lake), very beautiful with its tree-clad islands and background of mountains. On the shore of the lake we came

Bad Aibling (1936). The Olympic Games were being held in Berlin.

to the Lambach Haus, where we abandoned the cycles for half an hour while we took refreshment in the shade of the overhanging trees. The Lambach Haus was a magnificent building, the whole of the front being decorated with beautiful frescos, while three musicians entertained us and one of them could yodel a treat!

At Traunstein we turned south towards the mountains, and by a roughish road continued into Siegsdorf, where with seventy miles to our credit, we decided to stay the night.

We took our meal while listening to the talk of a group of Bavarians. Needless to say, we couldn't understand them and even when they tried to converse with us, little headway was made. To everything that was said we just answered 'Ja', until a puzzled look told us it should have been 'Nein'.

Next morning it was raining heavily. It's funny how much worse it seems to have to start in the rain, rather than have to endure it later. Anyhow, we donned our capes and splashed off down the village street. We noticed that the locals donned a heavy cloth cloak, with hood attached, to protect them from the elements.

According to our original plan we should have continued south into the mountains and the Austrian border at Melleck, but now we had second thoughts and decided to retrace our tracks to Traunstein, then ride east to Salzburg, which seemed to offer some good prospects for the cameras.

In due course we arrived at the frontier at Saalbruck and, having been relieved of our money declaration forms, we crossed over into Austria. Triptiques were stamped, passports examined and stamped and we were at liberty to explore Austria to our hearts' content. One of the customs officials told us, in English, that it had been raining on the Gross Glockner Pass for the past three weeks, and that on the previous day there had been a blizzard! As we planned to cross over the Gross Glockner the next day, you can imagine how we received this news. It seemed that the weather had been consistently bad throughout the summer, but, as one member of the party argued, it was bound to stop raining sometime! And with this consoling thought, we advanced. We now had to ride not on the right hand side of the road, as we had since leaving Munich, but on the left, and this instruction was attached to every telegraph pole – 'Links fahren', we were instructed!

At last we came to Salzburg and, it being about lunch-time, we sought out a restaurant, where an amiable little Austrian, who had been for some time in Bradford and spoke good English, was able to supply our needs without the need for the usual phrase-book. Then, in the rain, we set forth to see what Salzburg had to offer. We noticed that one and all carried umbrellas – even the cyclists. To see them manipulating their cycles over the greasy roads, and across tram-lines, with the umbrellas poised overhead, was a sight for sore eyes!

By this time we were, truly, soaking wet, so we wandered back to the restaurant where another coffee helped prepare us for the road once more.

An hour's riding brought us to another frontier, and we were on German soil for the second time that day. Our stay in Germany, this time, was to be of very short duration; indeed, we could, without much exertion, have ridden across the neck of Germany which had to be crossed, before sunset.

However, we passed through Bad Reichendal and, making excellent progress, came to Mauthausl.

Further on we came upon a party of boys, who turned out to be from Wakefield Grammar School and who were on holiday with a couple of masters and two old boys. They were particularly friendly and we had a long discussion, exchanging our respective experiences. It transpired that they were staying at a hotel-cum-youth hostel at Scheizlreuth, just a mile or so down the road and, learning that there were beds available, decided to try our luck.

This didn't turn out to be as simple as we had hoped and it seemed impossible to make our requirements known to the lady in charge, until the leader of the boys arrived on the scene, and with his perfect know-ledge of German, quickly made known our wants, and beds were secured. What a wonderful thing is education!

Later we all sat down to a very much appreciated meal after our day of riding in the rain. Following dinner we were entertained by a party of German girls, members of the Hitler Youth Movement, on a walking tour of Bavaria. With their leader playing a guitar, they started a sing-song and of course we joined in, after a fashion, while later on they sang several English songs, and in English too! Later in the evening several of the locals entered and a dance got under way, with the jovial, red-faced little Bavarian innkeeper playing an accordion. The village policeman, one of the jolliest chaps I have ever met, was the organizer. All that was in 1936 – I wonder what became of them all?

Next morning the sun shone from a cloudless sky, and after we had said 'good-bye' to our new friends, we were away, and heading for the border. A few miles of good road brought us to the frontier at Melleck, and for the second time, we entered Austria. We crossed the Stein Pass immediately before reaching the Customs House, though compared with what we hoped to see later on in our tour, this was not taken seriously. We passed through the little village of Unken and then yet another small pass was negotiated, the Knie.

By now we were running into the mountains, which rose higher and higher about us as we approached. Lofer was a typical Austrian village, surrounded by massive peaks, and with its pretty little white-washed church and people in typical Austrian costume was, perhaps, the most interesting place so far.

Turning west on leaving Lofer, we ascended the Strub Pass at 2,257 feet, and in doing so we passed from the province of Salzburg into Tirol. The Strub Pass did not hinder us and after riding through the village of the same name, we came to Waidring, yet another charming place, where we turned south along a by-road.

This by-road, which we had been recommended not to miss, took us to two delightful villages, Winkel and St. Adolari, then, riding by the shore of a blue lake, we came to St. Ulrich, where, as we were by this time ready for a meal, we sought food and refreshment in the village *Gasthaus*.

At Schwent we turned our wheels east once more, soon finding ourselves climbing steeply by a narrow track, no more than six feet wide. We were convinced we were on the wrong road, but couldn't understand where we had gone wrong. However, we continued, with the intention of getting our bearings when we reached the highest point of the road, which would, almost certainly, give us a view of the valley. A village hove in sight and this proved to be Hochfilzen, and as this spot was on our route, we were, apparently, on the right road after all.

At Hochfilzen we had reached the summit of the pass, the Greissen, at a height of 3,176 feet, and for the next few miles we free-wheeled happily. The road surface was not of the best, unfortunately, and after reaching the floor of the valley, Ken sustained a puncture.

After passing through several small villages we arrived at the main road, then continued to Zell-am-See, which is one of those super-tourist resorts which we detest, so it did not take long deciding to proceed until we found a quieter spot higher up.

As we were about to move out of Zell-am-See, we met three cyclists from Coventry and, as they were heading up the Glockner the next day, even as we planned to do, we hoped to see more of them.

We left the shore of the Zeller See, a large lake adjoining the town of similar name, and from 2,487 feet commenced a steady grind on a fine wide road.

We were on the road which led up to the Gross Glockner Pass and, as we all appeared to be in excellent form, we made grand progress, so much so that we decided to continue fourteen miles to Ferleiten, where the Glockner commenced in real earnest. Our idea was to get a flying start next morning, if such were possible on a one in seven gradient. At Fusch we were 2,648 feet above sea level and we finally reached Ferleiten as evening commenced to fall, with 3,776 feet beneath us.

We were in the act of putting our stock query concerning accommodation to the proprietor of the Tauern Hotel, when two chaps arrived, complete with ice-axes and ropes. Over our evening meal they told us that they hailed from Manchester, and they had been a full week on the Glockner Pass waiting for an opportunity to scale

The Gross Glockner Pass.

the Glockner peak. They had been prevented from doing so by the atrocious weather; indeed, that day they had been caught halfway across a glacier by a blizzard, and a photographer who was with them at the time, had slipped twenty feet down a crevasse. They told us this in a most matter-of-fact manner. 'Most amusing,' said one of them. 'This photographer chap slipped down a crevasse – matter of twenty feet. Frightful fun getting him out. Couldn't reach him, of course, with our axes, so we dug steps from the top, and he did likewise from the bottom, until we could hook axes and hoist him up. Poor chap – he was scared.'

After hearing several tales of this stamp, our own activities paled into insignificance.

Thursday saw us up fine and bright, eager to learn of the wonders of the renowned Glockner Pass. We wended our way out of the village and reached the toll house. Now, at that time, each cyclist had to pay one Austrian (9d.) schilling for the privilege of using the Glockner road, but in view of the fact that a motorist had to pay eight schillings for each seat in his vehicle, well, it didn't seem so bad!

We moved off and immediately the road took on an upward trend of one in six, so after a few hundred yards, we decided to walk for a while. As the scenery was so utterly absorbing I think this was the right decision, as it allowed us to take greater note of the surroundings, and shoot off numerous photographs.

The morning gave promise of turning into a glorious day as clouds of mist were swirling across the peaks, thinning every minute, while the sun shone with real brilliance. The first mile or so did not offer any scenery or particular merit, and I was beginning to feel just a trifle disappointed, but thought that surely better things were before us. And so it proved. In giant loops the road worked its way up into the mountains, and when we had covered several miles, we looked back to see Ferleiten nestling in the valley, far, far below, with the movement of people plainly visible though thousands of feet down.

The scenery was improving all the time, and we revelled in the wonders about us: the brave snow-flecked peaks standing resolute among the swirling white clouds; the white streaks of waterfalls descending from the snow caps, and the scarred and scratched grey peaks falling to the bright green of the valley, patched with dark masses of fire. This was good, the type of scenery I live for. Needless to say, photographs were the order of the day, and the only thing that prevented us from keeping the camera shutters working, was the matter of finance!

The gradient was still as severe as when we left Ferleiten, but we were, by now, feeling very fit, thanks to the glorious atmosphere, and the delightful surroundings.

When we reached the Edelweiss-Spitz Hotel, we adjourned for lunch, which we took in the open at a height of 8,000 feet. Where we were seated we were sheltered from the wind by the hotel and the sun was so strong that it almost burned our skin, but round the angle of the wall a cold wind blew. From where we sat we looked across an immense, barren, rocky valley to a positive sea of blue peaks, white flecked with snow, like waves on a storm-swept sea.

Suddenly, a great commotion arose; everyone seemed to be dashing around, getting in each other's way, stumbling and falling over one another. What on earth was going on? Then a young Austrian told us that the clouds had moved off the Glockner peak which stood revealed for the first time in three weeks! Were we in luck? In what seemed no time at all, twenty photographers were standing in a row to get shots of this shapely, conical, snow-enshrouded peak.

From where we stood it was impossible to decide what course the road took; several stretches were on view, but for the life of us we couldn't decide which was coming and which was going, so to speak. We resumed and soon passed the monument erected to the memory of Dr Dolfus, a highly respected Austrian at the time, although this respect was later refuted by Adolph Hitler. We swept down into the valley and, riding by a chilly mountain lake, commenced the final long climb to the summit. Hundreds of cyclists must have passed over the Gross Glockner that day, and we kept meeting them – lone cyclists with heavy roadster type cycles and enough luggage to last the rest of their days; parties of two to six on all manner of machines – Germans, Austrians, Italians, French, Dutch and English. On the whole the continental cycles seemed to be much inferior to our own. True, we saw several super racing models, usually French or Italian, these being complete with derailleur gears, alloy bars, stem, pedals etc. and sprint

The Glockner Peak.

wheels (with tubular tyres) but these hardly seemed suitable for touring in such a district.

The most popular touring machine on the continent, seemed to be a heavy roadster fitted with that old abomination the plunger brake, which as you probably know operates on the *tread* of the front wheel! Any defect in the front tyre could prove disastrous. No wonder some cyclists preferred to stuff bunches of fir twigs between the crown and the front tyre. We saw several, thus equipped tearing down the pass. I don't know how they got away with it!

In due course we came to a tunnel and plunged into its gloomy interior for a hundred yards or so before emerging into the sunshine, seemingly ten times as bright as ever. Onward once more, ever upward, until yet another tunnel had to be negotiated, and this time our way was illuminated by electricity, to guide us to the distant daylight.

But this time we came out right at the summit of the pass, for actually the final tunnel took us through the strip of rock which separates the north side from the south. And how different everything was on the south side. Instead of the road and the surrounding mountain slopes, tending in an upwards direction, all was now reversed, and from the grey peaks, the mountains dropped rapidly away to the fir trees far below.

Away we sped, joyously swerving and twisting in our downward plunge, the barren greyness of the bare rock giving way to the green pine-clad slopes, while the majestic peaks reared higher as we sped along. We came to a T-junction from where the road snaked out along the mountainside before plunging down into the valley and to Heiligenblut, visible to us, its church and buildings mere specks, thousands of feet below.

From this point, however, a road ran away to the right, through pine forest, again to climb into the peak bound upland to Franz Joseph and on to the Pasterzen Glazier. This road was a dead end, but we had heard such glowing reports of the wonders of this region, that we decided that we would journey along it, and retrace our steps next morning.

How glad we were that we had made this decision when the glories of the area unfolded before us. From where we left the junction, we climbed steadily along a good surfaced road, through pine-forests high above the valley. Loop after loop we accounted for until we came to a mountain *Gasthaus*, and here sought accommodation. All was well so, having disposed of our cycles, we ordered a meal for a later hour, and set off on foot for the Franz Joseph Haus Glacier. Our mountaineer friends of the previous night had told us of the thousands of alpine flowers to be found in the area and, indeed, had shown a tin full of specimens they had collected. Well, we found the roadside was carpeted with the blues, reds and pinks, making a glorious picture with the rearing peaks for background. How fortunate we were to witness this beautiful sight.

We strolled along admiring the marvellous peaks which the evening sun was now touching with pink, until we came at last to the glacier. The sun, low down, was sending long blue shadows across the scored and crevassed ice of the glacier, and made a memorable scene. By a precipitous path, we made our way down onto the ice, and had the interesting experience of walking on ice hundreds of feet thick and goodness knows how many years old.

As the sun dipped behind the Gross Glockner peaks, the air became bitterly cold and we were glad of the exertion needed to regain the road.

It was pitch dark by the time we arrived back at the *Gasthaus*, but we had to wait some considerable time for our meal, which can be a serious matter when you are already ravenous! At long last we were seated in the dining room, watching, with envious eyes, other tourists devouring large helpings of Frankfurt sausages. One chap in particular seemed to be obtaining especial enjoyment from his repast and eventually Ken said to him, after long thinking about his speech, 'Es ist gut,' to which he replied, after licking his lips and smiling broadly, 'Ja! Bloody good.' He told us that he had received his 'English' education in Bradford, as had the restaurant proprietor in Salzburg.

Having, eventually, devoured our frankfurters with great relish, we went to bed with the temperature down below freezing point but, of course, we were then at an altitude of 8,000 feet, which, when you think about it, is twice as high as Ben Nevis!

Once more the mist was blowing off the peaks as we breakfasted next morning, giving promise of more glorious weather to come. We were, indeed, in luck. Here the weather had been atrocious right through the summer, like a prolonged winter, and then the very day we arrived, the skies were magically cleared and the sun shone.

After shooting off a few exposures of the surroundings, we secured our cycles and set off on the great downward swoop to the point at which we had branched off for the Pasterzen Glacier. How different everything appeared in the morning light. The lighting was, of course, the reverse of that of the night before; consequently it produced an entirely different aspect.

Before continuing our downward plunge, we stood for some time admiring the exquisite mountain scenery about us. To us, Heiligenblut seemed only just beyond arm's length, but we knew that actually it was three thousand feet below and about five miles by road. Remounting, we ascended for a few hundred yards, then commenced the descent: a

delightful straightaway run at breath-taking pace. Down below, Heiligenblut drew nearer and nearer, until we realised that we were passing
it, overhead so to speak and, continuing a mile down the valley, we
turned and rushed back into this charming mountain village.

It is remarkable that no details seem to be published regarding gradients
etc. of the Glockner, but on the Ferleiten side gradient is said to be one
in seven. When it is realised that this is maintained almost the whole
way up, the severity of the climb can be imagined. We found it steeper
than the Slelvio and, though the road itself is nothing like so remarkable,
at the same time the views from the Edelweiss-Splitz and the Franz Joseph
Haus are extremely fine.

Heiligenblut has a very beautiful church, and down in the crypt we
found a most remarkable model of the village and the surrounding mountains, as they were in the fifteenth century.

In the village store, where we had gone for post-cards, I perfected
my speech, after much argument and perusal of the phrase book, thus:
'Haben Sie post-carte?' or something like that and the assistant replied,
'Oh yes, postcards, certainly, help yourself.' Well, that's how it goes!

Further hectic miles and the road more or less levelled out in the
valley, and we continued south with the mountains high on either hand.
Mind you, the road surface was atrocious, being absolutely chockful of
pot-holes, and loose and dusty. Road-making appeared to be in progress,
so it is possible that future generations may have seen an improvement
in this road from Heiligenblut to the Iselberg Pass.

As we sat under the trees, lunching at the village *Gasthaus* at Winklern,
the sun blazed down, but we noticed nasty-looking wisps of grey cloud
sailing across the sky from the west, and though we told ourselves that
what rain might be on its way would blow over, sad to relate it didn't
do so, and after a long, low-gear climb through the pine trees of the
Iselberg Pass we were greeted by the first splashes of rain as a mighty
thunderstorm swept over the towering peaks – even as we made the
summit. With lightning flaring and thunder rolling angrily round the
peaks, the road was soon turned into a river by the torrential rain, so
we adjourned to a large barn and, seated on piles of hay, watched the
storm play itself out.

The sky was still heavy when we resumed our ride, though the rain
had stopped. Almost immediately we were rushing downhill over the
treacherous surface of the rain-soaked road, sliding almost broadside round
the corners, sloshing along the straights and, in general, having a really
hectic time.

All in one piece, we eventually arrived at Dolsach at the foot of the pass, and turned west along a good surface to Lienz, with the Lienz Dolomites rearing up to the south, the battlemented peaks tearing the racing clouds.

Lienz we found to be a fair-sized village, very clean, with fine wide streets flanked by colourful buildings, and it was here that we met once more, the tandem couple we had seen on the Glockner. It was from them that we learned our first news of the world since leaving home. It seemed that they had purchased a London *Daily Mail*, from which it seemed that things were not looking too good. in fact, as it was put to us, 'Europe was on the verge of war'. You will remember that it was eventually postponed for a couple of years!

Needing more Austrian money we visited the bank, where, like nearly everyone in Austria, the bank clerks wore national costume. We had even seen commercial travellers strutting about in their leather shorts and little grey jackets.

We left Lienz behind and, nicely clear of the last building, felt the spotting of rain on us once more. As it developed into a steady downpour we had no option but to 'cape up'. The ensuing ride was a dreary business, with the rain continuing, so when, some time later, at Strassen, we espied a sign which read 'Jos Burlers *Gasthaus*' we there and then voted to call it a day.

We had a long wait for our evening meal, and we were beginning to think that this was usual in Austria, but it proved worth waiting for. Later on, the landlord and his daughter got hold of one of our phrase books, which they used in reverse and we were able to correct their pronunciation. Then the young lady and an Italian chap treated us to a duet, while later still a gramophone was dragged out of the lumber room, cobwebs dusted off, and we were entertained by the playing of various antiquated records. And so to bed.

As we peered hopefully out of our bedroom window next morning, we were pleased to see that the rainclouds had been swept away and the sun shone on the green of the valley, while through the white mists blowing across the hillsides, a tiny church perched amid new snow. Yesterday's rain had been snow on the hills. Group photos having been taken, it was considered sufficiently warm for the stowing away of jackets, etc. and then, away we went, still climbing slightly, but with the improved weather, better able to appreciate our surrounding.

Sillian was the last village in Austria, and a little later we reached the frontier, where, having been duly passed out of Austria, we introduced ourselves to Mussolini's underlings! The soldiers looked very picturesque in their grey-green uniforms, with Boy Scout hats, pinned up at one

side, and long feathers projecting rearwards! At last we were in Italy, and
not so very far from the main objective of our tour – the Dolomites.

The scenery was only moderate for the first few miles, but we knew
that before many hours mighty peaks would come along to delight us.
San Candido was alive with country folk and tourists, while a squad of
soldiers trailed through the town, *en route* for the mountains and manoeuvres. Dobiacco, three miles further on, we found to be the scene of
great excitement, though the reason was not apparent; crowds of people
pushed and jostled one another, shouting and gesticulating, so we had
difficulty forcing a passage through to the open road beyond. At 4,000
feet and climbing steadily, we rode beside the Lago di Dobiacco, whose
green waters looked very inviting to our swimmers. In the heat of the
sun, which was now nearly overhead, we pedalled on up the Landro
Valley, the surroundings getting more and more attractive all the while.

We came to the site of the pre-war village of Landro. Of this once
flourishing village, all that remained was a mass of crumbling masonry
and the hollow shell of a church. We were told that the Austrians, to
whom this area belonged prior to the Great War, blew up the village to
clear the way for their long-range artillery, which was unsuccessful against
the advancing Italians. How diabolical that such magnificent scenery
should be the scene of conflict. Even the mountains themselves suffered,
some mighty peaks being made unrecognisable through having pieces
blown off by artillery fire. Mountaineers, returning after the war, had to
find new ways up the peaks.

With the mighty blue, battlemented and crevassed mass of the Monta
Christalla range rising up before us, we were well and truly entering the
Dolomite region. The Dolomites are a range of mountains quite apart
from any other, and the shapes which the jagged peaks assume are nothing
short of fantastic. The Lago di Landro, perfectly calm and blue-green in
colour, made a charming foreground for the lofty peaks.

We rode into Carbonin and took lunch on a huge veranda, while
gazing out on the beauties of the Croda Rossa peaks, their serrated mass
blotched by red, blue and green.

By now, some adventurous instinct had taken hold of John, and he
announced his intention of leaving us, to make a wild dash across the
mountains and include the Stelvio Pass in his itinerary, his intention being
to meet up with us later at the summit of the Brenner Pass.

When we took the Col St. Angelo road out of Carbonin, John rode
off direct for Cortina. We climbed steadily, but the views presented to
us as we ascended amply repaid any physical effort; the gradient was not
all that severe, and intelligent use of the gear lever aided us considerably.

When we were well above the valley, a backwards glance gave us a wonderful view of the Croda Rossa, its peaks rearing up to the fleecy white clouds which blew over it. The summit was reached at 5,700 feet with the Monta Christalla on our right and the Monta Piana on the left.

Our road led downward for a few miles, before climbing over the Tre Croci Pass, and eventually to Cortina. We sped down through the pines, gloriously happy in the fine air and brilliant sunshine. A spell of climbing brought us to the Tre Croci Hotel which marked the summit of the pass at 5,879 feet; and now commenced a truly magnificent descent. Mile after mile, we hurtled along, easing up on the corners, to accelerate rapidly, with the wind in our ears, down the next grade. Unfortunately the surroundings offered so many irresistible invitations to the photographer, that the descent had to be punctuated by sudden halts while some outstanding scene was put on record. Dan caused concern, and then amusement, when after 'singing' his way around several hairpins, he met one that got the better of him, and after careering round the outer rim of the spooned out-corner, he finally dropped from sight over the edge. Fortunately, very fortunately, he landed on a grassy slope.

Cortina received us down a long, thrilling, dead straight, slope, and what a picture it made as we descended, with its cluster of colour-washed buildings dominated by the high tower of the church, the whole backed by the chiselled mass of the Togana peaks standing bare above the pine-clad lower slopes.

The sun was, by this time, getting low, and the mountains were taking on their evening tinge of pink, so our original plan of continuing over the Falzarego Pass was abandoned and we sought beds in Cortina.

Now Cortina, in common with Kandersteg and Val Iseran, has become a world-famous winter sports centre, but even in 1936, and in summer it was extremely busy. So much so that we had tried our luck at six hotels before being accepted at the Algergo Ponte Chiusa, and then only after pleading with the manager for nearly half an hour! Actually, the hotel was full but he finally agreed to rig up beds in the dining room!

We had a wonderful meal, and then, the dining room having been cleared, we finally retired for the night, although we did not retire to orthodox beds. Several beds had been placed together, and we were to sleep across them!. Thus the one bed accommodated the five of us! However, we had no problem sleeping – that's one of the wonderful things about cycling; after a day on the cycles one can sleep anywhere.

An easy climb took us high above Cortina, and after accounting for three hairpins, we passed over the terminus of the Cortina Mountain Railway, and continued by a comfortable gradient. Indeed, we found that all the Dolomite roads had been recently rebuilt, and were splendidly graded with excellent road surfaces. The mighty Tolfana Rock wall towered up above us, 11,000 feet, standing high above the belt of dark green pines – great masses of pinkish stone of every conceivable form – sometimes tapering, slender pinnacles, sometimes solid fortress-like blocks.

Following a nine-mile climb, during which we rose from 4,000 feet to just on 7,000, we reached the summit of the Falzarego Pass, and halted at the hotel for refreshments before taking the downward plunge. The sky was just an unbroken expanse of blue, the air clean and pure, while looking across the peaks, the eye travelled right away to the horizon, and all was clean-cut. Close by the summit rose the isolated peak of Sasso di Stria, like a small version of the Matterhorn, standing guard over the pass.

An easy gradient and an excellent road surface enabled to us to burn up the eight miles down to Andrez – swinging away from side to side, and so on down into the valley.

On a ledge on the mountainside, wonderful views rewarded us as we rode from Andrez to Pieve, with the Andrez valley opening up to the south – little clustered villages, strung together by a thread of white road, while in the distance rose the shattered cone of Monte Forca.

We found a little restaurant where we lunched, while in the next room half-a-dozen Italians were gathered. The noise those six made was unbelievable – they yelled and screamed at one another at the top of their voices, all shouting, no one listening. Several times we were sure murder was being committed, but investigations revealed that all were, apparently, still the best of friends.

Continuing up the valley, we were hailed by a young cyclist in need of assistance. Speaking a little English, he told us that he lived in Vienna, and though only a lad of sixteen, he had left home for a week's cycle-camping tour – on a full roadster machine loaded up to the sky with gear, and fitted with that old abomination, the plunger brake. But that lad was tough, as he had, according to our calculations, covered over three hundred miles in three days!

We left the Austrian lad and continued to Arabba, and here decided that instead of proceeding direct over the Pordai Pass to Canazie, we would substitute three passes, the Campo Lungo, the Gardena, and the Sella.

We climbed out of Arabba on a road which carried us up high above the valley, before finding a gap in the mountain wall. The Campo Lungo hadn't the quality of the previous passes but still it was interesting, as indeed were all roads in this amazing district. The summit came at just under 7,000 feet, and then followed a delightful free-wheel run down into the valley at Corvara.

We were sailing along, taking the hairpins in thrilling succession, when we received the shock of our lives! On rounding one particular bend, the front man, Ken, gave a yell of warning, and the next instant there appeared an *army tank*, grinding its way round the corner, forcing us out onto the extreme edge of the precipice. Well, we made it somehow, and then saw another half dozen of these things coming up the pass, followed by armoured cars, evidently going up the mountains for practice.

With the Campo Lungo accounted for we turned east at Colfosco, under the shadow of the shapely Sas Songher peaks, but almost immediately, we ran into another section of what turned out to be the famous Italian Alpinist regiment on manoeuvres, and as we urged our cycles up the stiffish gradient, we saw scores of tanks and armoured cars hidden among the pine trees. We proceeded, to the cheers of the soldiers!

It was now that we commenced our assault on the Gardena Pass, and found this to be the stiffest since the Glockner. It was not long before we found ourselves strung out over a considerable distance, and with the road zig-zagging violently on its upward journey, we appeared to have a hairpin each. But the scenery was simply exquisite, so first one then another would be hopping off his cycle as some particular scene caught his eye. We had long left the trees behind when we did, eventually, climb up onto the plateau on the summit. A brief rest and we were climbing up the mountainside to admire the amazing views around us.

The sun was getting low and again the mountains were taking on their multi-colours – greens, blues, purples and reds – all delightfully merged, while the atmosphere was so clear that every little detail was visible on the stupendous, shattered peaks, which rose, like natural castles, into the evening sky. These incredible peaks and the unbelievable colours are a feature of the Dolomites. We witness certain scenes in our cycling careers which we will never forget, and this, surely, will be one that everyone will think about as his mind goes back over the glories that cycling has made possible.

To the north rose the black silhouette of the Comme Rossa Peaks, jagged as the teeth of some gigantic saw, while to the south, the 10,000 ft. mass of the Sassa di Lago dominated the pass.

The sky was beginning to darken by the time we were able to tear ourselves away from this glorious scene but, mounting our cycles, we were soon hurtling off downward towards the distant valley. From 7,000 feet we descended for five miles to the junction of the Sella Pass. By this time we felt we should be thinking about accommodation for the night,

The Dolomites.

unless we were to spend the night up in the mountains, so we continued down into the Gardena Valley, confident there would be a hotel not far away.

After a mile or so of descent we found our hotel, the Rifugio Plan di Gralba, and fortunately they could find us accommodation, although the news that we had to wait a couple of hours for our evening meal was a bit of a body blow, as we were ravenously hungry. We filled in the waiting time by watching a game of skittles. This game is very popular in Italy, and almost every hotel seemed to have its skittle alley.

At long last, our meal was ready and we were confronted by a huge dish, three feet by eighteen inches, piled high with steaming hot spaghetti, over which was poured tomato sauce. Now some of the party liked this spaghetti, others did not, but for those that liked it there was a never ending supply. All manner of other eatables were provided and altogether we enjoyed an excellent meal. It seemed to please the Italians immensely to see us wolfing down their spaghetti. Incidentally, when we came to settle up next morning, we were only charged 6s. each for dinner, bed and breakfast.

We had only accounted for forty miles that day, but while crossing the three mighty passes we had seen some of the most delightful scenery that we had ever been fortunate enough to encounter.

The next morning, Monday, dawned fine, as had its predecessors and, climbing steadily, we came to the road junction we had left the night before, and so started on the Sella Pass. We were soon above the pine-trees, and backward glances revealed the Comme Rossa Peaks, while above towered the mass of the Sella Group.

A man on horseback astonished us by taking his horse straight up the mountainside, ignoring the road altogether. He eventually reached the summit long before we pedalled up the last rise, although the poor horse was sweating profusely and breathing heavily, while our cycles didn't appear to be any the worse for the climb!

There was obviously much to be seen from the summit and, neglecting our cycles for half an hour, we scrambled up onto a little plateau, where we were better able to feast our eyes on the glories about us.

From where we stood, a rocky basin separated us from the magnificent Sassa Lungo Peak, 10,329 feet, yet so clear was the atmosphere, combined with the vast size of the peaks, that it seemed we only had to stretch out our arms to touch them, as they rose crinkled and jagged into the blue, with plumes of white clouds caught to their summits.

The mountains of the Dolomites are composed of magnesium lime-stone, we learned, and consequently, are continuously crumbling into dust. With a strong wind, this is blown off the peaks and settles in the crevasses round the base, or on ledges. This has every appearance of being snow, indeed it is so much like snow that one often has difficulty in distinguishing the two. Without moving from our position we turned to look south, and the view took in the road leading up to the inevitable hotel, which stood at the summit, before sweeping left to work its way along a shoulder of the Sella Mountain Group, and so disappear into the pine trees below.

An immense valley lay before us, while in the distance, awe-inspiring against the light, rose the incredible bulk of the Marmalade Mountain, 11,000 feet and capped by eternal snow. From where we stood to the peak of the mountain was seven miles.

I had expected great things from the Dolomites. I had read about them, heard of other's experiences in this country of crazy peaks, and had long looked forward to finding myself among such celebrated delights. And now I stood in the very heart of the mountains I had dreamed of visiting, and I saw splendours even surpassing the vivid pictures of my imagination.

But, as with all beauty, it simply cannot be described by mere words, nor by photographic reproduction.

Time moved on, and we joyously remounted our cycles for the hair-raising descent to Canazie. We hurtled down the mountainside, snaking deep down into the pines. To free-wheel rapidly, for mile after mile, in such surroundings is a delight indeed. We came to a little lake, clear, green and inviting, so much so, that Dan and Fred stripped − and in they went. Of course, having gone so far, they had to carry the thing to the bitter end and tried to convince us that the water was beautifully warm, and that we were missing the treat of our lives. Their blue bodies and chattering teeth, however, did not back up their story, and we refused to be tempted.

Resuming, we reached the point where the Pordoi road joined to Sella, and, still on a downward grade, sailed along to Canazie. From 7,200 feet at the summit of the Sella we had descended to 4,200 feet at Canazie.

We lunched at a restaurant, styled the Villa Aurora, or rather in the adjacent tea-garden. The sun blazed down, as usual, and burned our arms and legs, but out of the shelter, a cool wind blew. We were entertained during our meal by a party of Italian students, one of whom played a mandolin, and then, on wheeling our cycles out onto the road, we once again met the tandem couple, and heard the news of the last few days.

It appeared that the World War had been postponed!

We left our friends for the last time and soon came to the little village of Gries, and then continued up the Val Fassa, through Campitello and Mazzin to Perra.

It was at Perra that Dan decided that he wanted to buy a stamp for a post-card, so, supplying himself with the necessary cash, he disappeared into the village post office. Half a hour later, he came scrambling down the mountainside with his 35 centessimi stamp clutched firmly in his hand. It turned out that the building he had entered, despite the fact that it was propped up by a pillar box, was not the post office, (the village hadn't one) and he had been sent, via the back door, to the next village, a mile up the mountain!

At Vigo di Fassa − a village possessing a large military barracks − we again turned our wheels into the mountains, for the Costa Lunga Pass, or as it was originally, the Karer.

As we left Vigo a thunderstorm blew up, so when we reached Valonga we decided to heave to, have a coffee at the village hotel, and wait while it blew over.

We got our coffee, but the final rumble was a long time in coming, and an hour later the thunder still rolled among the peaks, while the lightning streaked down, so we decided to stay there the night. Now when we had arrived we had thought the hotel looked somewhat dejected, so obviously we were not exactly charmed by the place, and by the time we left next morning, our opinion of it had sunk lower still. We had hoped that our initial impression would be groundless.

Well the rain did, eventually, cease, so ordering our meal for 8 p.m. we set off for a walk. Back at the hotel, we were shown into a cellar-like room, bare and cold, off which our bedroom opened (we were to sleep five in three single beds).

Night had fallen before there was any sign of our meal, and then plates of soup arrived – clear soup, or as we classified it, hot water. Then the inevitable spaghetti appeared, and I must say that was good – I suppose you can't go wrong with spaghetti. Except of course, that we seemed to have some difficulty charming the stuff with our forks! Then another, seemingly endless, wait and in came some sausages – fat, succulent and steaming. Excellent, we agreed. But, tragedy, there were only four; the fifth man had to have some sort of meat. Well Dan, hero that he is, immediately volunteered to have the meat, so the rest of us each secured a large, healthy-looking sausage. Now as soon as I stuck my fork into that sausage I knew that all was not well. A glance round the table told me that the other three were similarly affected. I took a bite at a small morsel, and tasted the worst taste of my life. Burning hot with unknown seasonings, this was nothing compared with the mixture of additional bad taste.

We ordered white wine, with which to drown the atrocious taste. Mind you the wine was pretty dreadful, but by comparison it was like nectar. Fred, without even spearing his, said 'Well, you chaps, I'm not jolly well tackling this,' and so saying, wrapped it up in a serviette and pocketed it.

Next morning, we resumed our onslaught on the Costa Lunga Pass; the weather was, as expected, fine and then, half a mile from the hotel, we pulled up by the roadside where an interesting ceremony took place. Fred carefully unwrapped his Italian haggis, and swung his arm, round and round, overhead, while the company chanted – five – four – three – two – one – and away it sailed, high into the air, to curve and plunge down into the tree-filled valley. A dull boom told us that it had gone to its last resting place.

The Costa Lunga was disappointing, and after a long, easy climb we arrived at the summit at 5,750 feet. Nor did we obtain the fine free-wheel run down the other side which we felt we had right to expect, as the surface of the road was very bad, and indeed as it was being reconstructed, was all ploughed-up and almost impossible to ride on at all.

We passed by the Karer See, a little lake which did not delay us long, and continued until, after a while, we found the surface a little better, though inches deep in dust which was raised in clouds by passing motor cars. We ran downhill through a great gorge, very deep and very narrow, with precipitous walls of rock rising from the roadside, which, being only twelve feet wide, and bordered on the other side by a surging river, made the passing of cars rather a thrilling business, especially as we could hardly see for the clouds of dust. At last, passing a castle perched high above the road, we met the main Brenner road, along which we turned to Bolzano.

By now we had dropped to a mere 860 feet, which was the lowest point since entering the Bavarian Alps by train, before Munich. But very warm it was in Bolzano, and after our dusty run we welcomed a clean-up before tackling lunch.

Very interesting, was our verdict on Bolzano, with its galleried streets – all shops being set far back from the road beneath these galleries. This was the largest town we had been in since Salzburg, and we spent some time inspecting the goods in the shops.

Eventually, the time came when we had to get back on the road, and on a rising gradient we continued steadily for the remainder of the day on the famous military road, the Brenner. There was nothing very interesting about the scenery; perhaps we had been spoiled by the splendours we had come to expect from this region. We proceeded up a very wide valley with patchwork slopes leading up to the mountains on either hand. A wide turbulent river roared downward, while the railway ran close to the road on its long journey to the summit.

It was a wise move when we decided to deviate from the main road into the village of Chiusa, which turned out to be a very interesting spot, with narrow, cobbled main street, picturesque buildings and iron-work signs.

Twenty-five miles beyond Bolzano, we cried enough at Bressanone. We were anxious to dispose of the rest of our Italian money as, according to the conditions under which traveller's cheques were sold in Italy at that time, no money could be taken out of the country, and we should reach the frontier next afternoon.

So we wheeled up to the largest hotel we could find, but to our disgust they were full up. And we tried six more hotels, each time receiving the same response, although it was never as easy as all that: sometimes it took half an hour to ascertain that there was no accommodation available, owing to our lack of knowledge of the language. We did eventually secure accommodation at a small though otherwise satisfactory hotel, somewhat off the beaten track.

In our pre-meal wandering, we stopped an old Italian ice-cream vendor, and made him understand that we wished to partake of his wares. Was he bucked? Three flavours for the price of one, he was offering, and he made a proper ceremony of plastering on the three colours, prior to handing over the finished product to each of us in turn, at the same

The Alpinist regiment on manoeuvres.

time raising his hat, most politely. It was the first time in my life that anyone had raised their hat to me!

Out on the main road, next morning, we were riding along on a slight down grade, when rounding a bend we came upon the most comical spectacle imaginable. About one hundred soldiers of the famous Italian Alpinist regiment on bicycles were coming towards us, reeling all over the road as they toiled up the slight rise. We couldn't help giving them a yell of encouragement as we passed.

At Mules we halted for lunch at an attractive hotel-cum-beer garden, and then on the road once more we made good progress, climbing, of course, continuously towards the summit of Brenner.

We came to Vipitene, another delightful village, all colour and animation. A high tower occupied the end of the village main street, and through this the road passed. This tower was coloured a delicate pink shade and carried a fine clock and sundial. These latter were works of art, coloured in red, blue, gold and white – extremely picturesque.

The altitude at Vipitine was 3,000 feet and, still rising, we came to Colle Isarco where a stall piled high with grapes caught our eye. They were almost giving them away so, having handed over a few lira, we staggered away with our arms full of bags of fruit. We tramped out of the village to find somewhere where we could consume some of our load, and before resuming our ride a British motor-cyclist touring with his wife pulled up for a chat. It seemed that, in a fortnight, we were the only British they had met.

And so came the summit of the Brenner Pass, 4,467 feet; not so high, nor so attractive as the Dolomites but, of course, of great international importance.

Before leaving home we had arranged to meet George and Rita Munson at Gries, three miles down the Austrian side of the Brenner, at 6 p.m. on Wednesday 12 August, at the Waldhem Hotel, where we had booked.

Well, we arrived at five o'clock and received a right royal welcome from the little Austrian proprietor, whilst also waiting was John. John had carried out his wish to 'do' the Stelvio, but had had to ride hard and continuously. He told us that he had been three days without food of a solid nature, owing to eating too much fruit, and this, combined with the heat he had encountered, had obviously told its tale!

At six o'clock George and Rita, who were riding tandem, arrived. And so, three thousand miles from home, we had met at the precise time planned. George had never been renowned for his time-keeping, which makes this all the more remarkable!

At the foot of the Stelvio Pass.

The Stelvio 'hairpins'.

When we had arrived, earlier on, one of the Austrian visitors at the hotel had acted as interpreter for us, and I dubbed him the British Consul. He was tickled to death at this, and when George and Rita arrived he said, 'Now if you want anything at all, just come to me. I am the British Consul by special appointment of your friend!'

We yarned until late into the night, telling of our respective adventures, while our Austrian friends told us of conditions in Austria: how the Italians were building huge forts on the mountainside overlooking the Brenner Pass, though, to use his words, 'Why they do this I do not know; Austria is too poor to cause any trouble.' The Austrians will never get over having part of their beloved country taken away from them by the Italians after the Great War. Even now, twenty years after the war, they still stuck to the old Austrian names for the villages, and if you mentioned a certain place by its Italian name, they would correct you.

Next morning we said goodbye to George and Rita and our Austrian friend, who was taking the train down to Innsbruck, twenty miles distant, and sailed away gloriously, down a steady gradient, just able to take the corners without braking, as we swept along. The scenery was interesting, but not to such a degree that we wanted to use our cameras, so the downhill run to Innsbruck was unbroken. The last stretch carried us along with a fine view of the town, with the mountains rising beyond.

We parked our cycles in the car park and set off on foot to explore the town, but had hardly gone fifty yards, when we were hailed by someone behind us. It was our Austrian friend from Gries smiling all over his face. We had accounted for the twenty-two miles in under the hour, without pedalling, and had beaten the train into the bargain!

I thought Innsbruck somewhat disappointing – were we expecting too much? Anyway, we explored it thoroughly, wandering down every little alley and side street in search of pictures; the Golden-Roofed House, the Arc de Triomphe etc. all received attention as did the fruit market. But I must tell you about John's sleeves. It seemed that he left his cycle when he went in search of a viewpoint, whilst on the Stelvio, and on his return he was horrified to see a cow in the act of chewing his jacket, which was strapped to his cycle. By that time the sleeves had completely disappeared, hence his odd appearance!

We lunched at Innsbruck, and then 'on, Stanley, on'. Down the valley to Zirl, and up into the hills once more, heading, of course, north.

George had told us a hair-raising tale of the Scharnitz Pass, the steepest he had ever done. We listened patiently to his story, given with the air of 'the man who has seen Everest', but when we actually encountered the Scharnitz, and its one in five gradient, we took back all we had said. The Scharnitz really was a terror, the toughest of the tour!

At Scharnitz village we re-entered Germany, and made further acquaintance with the swastika, and at Mittenwalde we cashed the remainder of our German travel cheques, before pushing on for a few more miles before dark. Mittenwalde we found very picturesque, as, indeed, were all the Bavarian villages, and full of tourists, most German, who at that time were not allowed to take holidays abroad!

Twelve miles riding and we came to the German Lake District, and after a few miles we rode by the side of the Walchensee, the largest German mountain lake – very fine in the evening light. We climbed to Kesselberg, 2,825 feet, and were greeted by a grand panorama, totally unexpected. From where we stood, the ground fell away rapidly to an extensive plain, across which the setting sun sent a beautiful golden mist. The run down from the Kesselberg was a sheer delight; mile after mile we coasted at twenty miles per hour. The road twisted and turned upon itself in its effort to find the easiest way down to the plain, while on a perfect surface we enjoyed it to the full.

We stayed the night at Kochel, and next morning cycled the remaining forty miles into Munich.

All afternoon we tramped round Munich, having first despatched our cycles through to Rotterdam, and obtained great entertainment inspecting, praising or criticising what we saw. We had supper in a typical Bavarian *Gasthof*. A band played cheerful music, while Storm Troopers, commercial travellers, even whole families sat round the tables, drinking beer or partaking of a full meal. What surprised us most was the amazing friendliness of the Germans. Several went out of their way to shake hands with us, when they knew we were English. But of course, these were the ordinary people!

Well, we left Munich and, after passing through Cologne, eventually reached Rotterdam. Then Hull, inevitably, where we split up and pedalled off to our respective homes, eager to tell the story of the amazing scenes that we had witnessed, and our adventures – exciting and humorous – on our journey to the country

WHERE THE MOUNTAINS BLUSH.

9

Awheel in Bosnia

Yugoslavia was the touring ground for a party of Hull members of the cyclists' Touring Club in August 1938, and this proved to be the last of a series of five pre-war continental cycling holidays.

But why Yugoslavia? Well, it was only after some interesting correspondence with Bernard Newman, a well-known cycling writer and lecturer, that the decision was made to explore this fascinating country. So I will endeavour to describe to you the amazing things we saw, and

our adventures, in what was, without doubt, the quaintest corner of Europe.

Our party consisted of Tom Clayton, Fred Greenway, Ron Oliver, Pip Pudsey, Dan Rowe and myself: all seasoned cycle tourists with numerous British tours, to say nothing of several on the continent, to their credit.

We travelled by train down to Harwich, then by steamer to Antwerp, before continuing by train to Munich. At Munich we had to make a further change of trains, then on to Zagreb and Sunja for a final change of trains – and a five-hour wait into the bargain. The train we had left resumed its journey to Istanbul. Now, on a branch line, the quality of the railway's rolling-stock deteriorated sadly, and the train which took us on the final stage of our journey provided little regard for passenger comfort! We shared a compartment with a be-fezed follower of Mohammed, several Serbs, a smart young lady in western dress – and a mad-man!

John Andrews and Fred Crooks had left Hull over a month previously on an extended tour of Europe, and had arranged to have a week with us. Well, when our train snorted into Bosanski Nova, concluding our 1,600 mile journey, they were waiting for us.

So far they had cycled through Germany into Czechoslavia – then through Austria (meeting two more Hull cyclists, Ken Howard and Wilf Rippon), and had reached Yugoslavia by way of Venice and Trieste. Unfortunately, they had arrived at Bosanski Nova without their cycles which had been mis-directed somewhere along the line, so they had to stay behind to await their arrival, with the promise to catch us up later.

The road which was to be ours to Banja Luka would have brought disgrace on any self-respecting English cart-track. The surface was composed of several inches of pure limestone dust, among which were concealed stones of varying sizes.

We came to Prijedor, and here could truly say that we had reached the east. As we entered the town a veiled woman shuffled by – a Moslem woman. She was garbed in a loose costume of grey material, with a hood carried over the head, while a black veil, or yashmak, completely obliterated her face.

Down on the river we saw boats fashioned out of tree trunks, while a regular procession of interesting characters passed by. A dark, be-fezed Moslem man wore strange, tight-fitting trousers, and led a couple of oxen; and there were more veiled women, and Christian girls whose brightly coloured dresses were in direct contrast to the clothes of the Moslems.

We rode on into the town and were at once surrounded by a dense mass of local people. When we made to take photographs, small boys

Moslem women in Prijedor.

took charge of our cycles, wheeling them alongside as we moved around. They were delighted to be able to assist 'des Ingleski' as they called us.

Everything was so unfamiliar, the primitive shops, the fierce heat of the sun, and Oh, the smell! Yugoslavia has a smell of its own – The National Smell of Yugoslavia. It seemed to be mainly derived from over-ripe fruit. Then the smells of Turkish coffee helped things along, while the whole was rounded off with decaying vegetables, sweating human bodies, pigs and garlic!

We went shopping for food for our picnic lunch, and the townspeople of Prijedor went with us. At the bakers, Dan and I went in to buy bread. Twenty locals teemed in after us. Outside a great crowd clamoured for admission, scared they would miss the fun. The shop-keeper was furious and, brandishing a carving knife, chased the intruders down the street. When he got back he had to fight his way into his own shop!

As we wended our way out of the town we saw many remarkable sights. On a low wooden truck, fitted with tiny, insecure wheels, sat an old beggar dressed in picturesque rags, who produced weird music from a strange instrument. A fair was in progress and we had to pick our way

'Pip' Pudsey and Ron Oliver in Prijedor.

The beggar (Sarajevo).

through throngs of people, past carts drawn by horses, oxen or donkeys, in charge of sleepy, often sleeping drivers, and through herds of cattle, sheep, pigs, goats, chickens and ducks – all registering their protest at the proceedings!

We eventually made it to the open road, but after riding some miles we realised that every living creature was asleep – except us! We travelled for mile after mile and never saw a soul. The road was still loose and dusty, and about seven miles an hour was all that was possible. (I used gears of 52 and 33 practically throughout the tour.)

Then, just to show how perverse the country could be, heavy clouds rolled up and we were in the middle of a fierce thunderstorm. But it was like no storm we had previously experienced – the lightning blazed away almost incessantly, while thunder rolled and groaned among the hills.

At long last we arrived at Banja Luka, a rather larger town than Prijedor, and here we stayed the night at the Hotel Bosna, on the recommendation of the Tourist Office.

Naturally, we could not leave Banja Luka without exploring its interesting streets and alleys, so we were up early next morning. Even so, we were long after the locals, who at 7.30 a.m. had, apparently, almost concluded their day's work!

Outside a coppersmith's establishment there were hung all manner of pots, kettles, pans and cauldrons – all of pure hand-beaten copper. A covered-in bazaar interested us, and here we watched cobblers, tinsmiths and basket makers working at their trades.

There were mosques to the right and left, but the most important was the Ferhad Pasha mosque. This was rather more elaborate than the smaller mosques, but the Moslem mosque is rarely ornamental.

But the time came for us to leave Banja Luka, and incidentally this stay had proved to be the most expensive of the whole tour, costing 10s. 6d. (or 53p as it would be today).

Just outside Banja Luka we came across a *barefoot* football match. When we were spotted, the match came to a halt – the lads found us much more interesting than a game of football. Fred issued a challenge to a game, and this was promptly accepted on the condition that we removed our shoes! NO MATCH.

Immediately after this incident we rode into a mighty gorge, and later found that this continued almost the whole way to Jajce, forty-five miles ahead, while roaring along throughout its length were the troubled green waters of the Vrbas. Beyond an occasional peasant's home we saw no habitation, and in fact there proved to be no hotel or restaurant for the whole of the ride. But we had the road to ourselves, and with the attractive scenery, this was a big compensation. Eventually, ever-increasing hunger caused us to lose interest in the scenery, and when we came upon a wayside house we approached it in the hope of obtaining some

The shopkeeper was angry.

food. They provided us with black bread but had nothing else in the way of food, while for a drink we had beer (or *peevo* as they call it), a very good fruit drink. The locals joined us at a table outside the house and, seeing the makings of a picture, I slipped away to fetch my camera, but on opening my saddle bag, I was horrified to discover the camera was not there. Then I remembered that I had left it near some bushes when the lads had bathed.

Well, Fred and Dan agreed to come back with me and we sped off for the five miles. The road was rough but the case was urgent – we must get back to my camera before someone else found it. We must have set up a new record for those five miles! We arrived at the spot where I distinctly remember having left my camera ... GONE! As we

A Bosnian windmill.

wandered, disconsolately, back to our bikes, a peasant chap approached
and indicated that we should follow him. After about half a mile he
entered a cottage and, to our delight, emerged with my camera – indicating that a small boy, who had appeared on the scene, had found it.
Quite a crowd gathered; where they all came from was a mystery, but
all seemed delighted to have returned my property. We gave them what
change we could rake up, wondering whether we had rewarded them
adequately. By the expressions on their faces, they were more than sat-
isfied.

I was able to take a photograph of the peasant at the entrance to his corn mill! The power, of course, was derived from the river.

Rejoining the rest of the party we proceeded towards Jajce, and towards threatening masses of cloud, away in the distance.

I was greatly fascinated by the stone-breakers we passed by the roadside. Like all we met in Yugoslavia they seemed to take life in an extremely leisurely fashion and the work was allocated like this: by each heap of stones three men squatted – *but*, only one worked at a time. Could it be that the supply of hammers was so restricted that only one could be supplied to each gang?

After watching the stone-breakers we made good progress before the thunderstorm burst. Deluges of rain descended, while vivid lightning blazed on the hills. We sheltered until the worst was over and then continued on a road transformed in minutes from a track six inches deep in white dust to a veritable glue-pot. Both Fred and Johbn had shed their rear mudguards somewhere in Czechoslovakia and were now treated to a steady stream of mud – right up their backs!

The deluge had other consequences. The rain-soaked mud and stones up the mountainside had slipped in places and trickled down onto the road, but after a few miles we came across a real landslide. Hundreds of tons of mud and stones had avalanched down the mountainside and crashed onto the road, completely blocking it to heavy traffic. Fortunately, we were able to climb over with our cycles and proceed. A little further on we were interested to see a gang of men forming timber-rafts of pine logs, which, as they were finished, were floated off down the river.

A tunnel we rode through was illuminated by acetylene lamps, and, emerging, we got our first glimpse of Jajce, built on a great egg-shaped hill and surmounted by a massive fortress standing velvet black against the red fire of a glorious sunset. We knew that we should find much to interest us in Jajce and we pushed on eagerly for the remaining miles.

We had difficulty in finding accommodation until a local youth volunteered his services and conducted us up steep narrow streets very nearly to the fortress itself. This chap was rather different from the others and spoke a little English, being dressed in western fashion. The building he took us to appeared to be a sort of hostel, but good beds were available although we were to feed elsewhere. We ran across him again later on, when he insisted on taking us to a coffee shop (or *kavana*) for coffee! To be honest we couldn't stand this Turkish coffee at any price. Quite a ritual, this coffee business, though. A tray was brought in bearing a tiny brass cup the size of a thimble together with a container of water. The purpose of the water was apparently to rinse out the mouth so that the full flavour of the coffee could be appreciated! We used the water to swill away the foul taste of the coffee – and then told our new friend how much we had enjoyed it!

We were up early next morning, eager to find the Pliva falls which we had heard so much about. They certainly proved well worth the effort. A great volume of water poured over a precipitous hundred-foot cliff, to smash into clouds of spray. Jajce is one of the most romantic and historically important places in Bosnia, and there are many traces of the Roman period. I was particularly anxious to get a photograph of the town's chief mosque, but had great difficulty in finding a decent viewpoint. When I finally got my picture, my feet were slowly sinking through the thatching on the roof of a chicken house!

The shoemaker (Jajce).

We found the open workshops of particular interest and a young shoe maker, patiently plying his needle, caught our eye. Patience seems to be one of the chief qualities of these Moslems. It is probable that the finished shoes are being displayed in my photograph of the local shoe shop, while the proprietor looks out in the hope of spying a prospective customer.

We made our way back to our sleeping quarters and asked for the bill. To our amazement the charge was less than 12d. *for the whole party.* Less than 2d. *each* or in today's currency, 1p. Is this a record?

We were sorry to leave Jajce, as there was certainly much still to be seen, but if we were going to complete our intended route we would have to be pushing on. So, riding at our new, customary 7 m.p.h. we steadily knocked back the miles, riding by the side of the hurrying green waters of the River Vrbas. After twenty miles we reached Donji Vakuf, and here purchased provisions for our picnic lunch, including bread which we obtained from a little baker's boy who seemed to be in sole charge of the open-fronted bakery. One commodity we failed to get was butter – they didn't seem to know what the stuff was!

When nicely out of the village we halted for lunch, seated by the roadside – a meal which was frugal to say the least.

The shoe shop (Jajce).

While lunching, peasants plodded by on their rather bony horses and one old chap pulled up for a yarn. At least, he stood grinning at us for about a quarter of an hour, neither he nor we being able to make ourselves understood.

At the foot of a set of zig-zags which was to take us up a small pass, we came upon two youths and a man selling little baskets of wild strawberries and raspberries, which they had gathered from the roadside. The baskets were made from pieces of bark from a tree and fastened by little splinters of wood. On the pass we overtook a man having a rather trying time driving a sow and a herd of piglets along the road.

Once at the summit, we found the road surface simply atrocious – by far surpassing anything we had previously experienced. Loose granite, in pieces as big as your fist, lay to a depth of six inches. We were forced to walk along this particular stretch of road.

As we approached Travnik we met folk apparently leaving the market, which we learned had been held in the town, and we noticed that many of the men wore red turbans. They rode on horseback or crowded together on the low carts peculiar to the district. These horsemen looked really dangerous brutes, the two massive pistols which some of them carried in their belts adding to their frightful appearance. Yet we found them quite friendly.

And so on into Travnik where we were able to fix up for the night at the Hotel Travnik. Over supper we were entertained by the landlord playing strange music on a harp, and then, with the meal a thing of the past, we took a stroll around the town. Travnik appeared to be some sort of military centre and we saw numerous army officers, white tunicked and carrying glittering swords – real picture book soldiers. It was amusing to see these hand-painted soldiers riding bicycles, with their swords hooked on the handlebars, and dangling alongside the front wheel.

Dinner, bed and breakfast cost us 3s. 4d. each, and this we found to be about the usual charge. Actually we were living on 5s. od per day, (25p).

As we passed the local butcher's on our way out of town, the butcher rushed out and indicated that he wanted his photograph taken – so, of course, I had to oblige. Whilst I was busy with the butcher, Fred Greenway was exercising his camera in the town square, but wherever he went he was accompanied by a small boy who carried a chair. Whenever Fred attempted to take a picture, this lad seated himself in the foreground!

On leaving Travnik we continued on the familiar dusty road, but after some miles Fred Crooks discovered that he was losing the soles of his shoes, so he returned to Travnik to have his repairs attended to at the little cobbler's establishment we had noticed. It was at about this time that John decided to sustain a puncture. So while John attended to his puncture and we waited for the return of Fred from the cobbler's the rest of us buried ourselves in the hedgeside, out of the fierce heat of the sun.

With our immediate problems sorted out, we continued steadily devouring the miles, the scenery being very pleasant with pine-covered hills on either hand, and mountains rising in the distance.

We were now within striking distance of Sarajevo, the capital city of Bosnia, and we pushed on eagerly so that we might reach the city while it was still daylight.

At a little place called Kiselisk we halted at an inn for a glass of lemonade, and the proprietor gave us, gratis, a glass of water from the local mineral spring – 'sour water' he called it! Further on we heard the peculiar wailing of the Moslem priest calling the faithful to prayer. We saw Moslems walking down the road to the service, and as it was Friday, the Mohammedan holy day, they were dressed in their best garb of white trousers and shirts with brilliantly coloured sashes around the waist, sometimes red, sometimes green. Occasionally we noticed a white turban round the usual red fez, and learned that this indicated that the wearer had made the pilgrimage to Mecca. This is every Mohammedan's ambition, of course, and the poorer of them often save up all their lives so that they can make the pilgrimage before they die.

Storms clouds gathered as we reached Sarajevo, and we rode on urgently so that we might reach the city before the drenching rains came down. On most evenings one of these storms would burst, though perhaps they had the effect of preventing the heat becoming absolutely unbearable. I really think that the glass of 'sour water' possessed amazing properties as we found ourselves getting along in fine style, and we eventually rode into Sarajevo at two o'clock, hours before we had expected. Incidentally, we noticed that the signposts were written in Cyrillic script, more than puzzling to us.

Entering Sarajevo from the west, I must say that we were at once disappointed – 'Just like any other modern city,' was our opinion. We rode down a wide asphalted road with super shopfronts on either side and neon signs galore. Clanging electric trams passed us and motor cars sped by. Then the streets became narrower, and the shops were of a more humble nature, though the trams persisted. Suddenly the trams had gone, and we found ourselves not in Europe at all, but in an Oriental market. We were in a dense jam of humanity – be-fezed and baggy-seated men, women in loose grey, hooded costumes. On either hand, instead of the modern city shop fronts and neon signs, were tiny wooden, open-fronted shops, hung with streamers of brightly coloured cloths and masses of shoes and sandals, carpets, fruit, jewellery and copperwork. We passed little *kabanas* where Moslems sipped their Turkish coffee. Over the tops of the shops white minarets towered, and the air was filled with the chatter of strange tongues.

So this was Sarajevo.

A lady assistant at the Putnik Tourist Office directed us to the Hotel Soko, and here we were made welcome. A good clean up and we were ready for the splendid meal that was provided.

Eager to make full use of the remaining hours of daylight, we were soon on our way and found our way to the Turkish market, where we saw hundreds of little stalls and open-fronted shops, and watched old Bosnians squatting on carpets, offering for sale the beautiful works of Oriental art, many-coloured tissues, metalwork and embroideries. We watched men making, by hand, knives of all shapes and sizes, with fine inlaid handles. Outside another shop a great piece of meat was being

The Turkish Market (Sarajevo).

roasted over a charcoal fire. We strolled down one street composed entirely of furrier's establishments.

Higher up the hill we saw grand white-washed houses, standing in beautiful gardens – the homes of wealthy merchants. Looking back, we gazed over the heart of Sarajevo, across the Turkish market to the ornamental Town Hall, and the river Miljacker.

The sun went down, darkness descended, and the little shops were shuttered up for the night. The Moslem hours of business are sunrise to sunset.

By six o'clock next morning, Pip and I were up and about, eager to exercise the cameras on the wonders of Sarajevo. We saw rickety houses with charming latticed windows and entrancing views looking across the hills draped in the morning mists. Descending to the lower parts we wandered into the market, and inspected stalls piled high, higgledy-piggledy, with a riot of colours and designs: picturesque slippers of red

The Princip Bridge (Sarajevo).

The curtain seller (Sarajevo).

or yellow leather, brass coffee services, filigree pipes, sashes in gorgeous red, yellow or gold.

We visited the state carpet factory and here were shown round by a tall Moslem. We saw girls in national dress, working at hand looms, turning out the most beautiful carpets. We climbed high out of the town, up a hillside, and viewed the town spread out over the valley, and lapping up the hills opposite. We saw countless minarets, like white candles, reaching up to the blue of the sky. We learned that in Sarajevo there were a hundred minarets, and that one-third of the population were Mohammedans.

The Town Hall was a fine building, and it was from this building that the Grand Duke Ferdinand rode in his carriage on that memorable day in June 1914 to meet his death at the hands of a crazy student. This incident was, of course, later used as an excuse for Austria declaring war on Serbia and, as everyone knows, the result was the Great War. Bosnia was at that time under the rule of the Austrians, who maintained that the student, Princip, was put up to do the murder by the Serbians. Princip then attempted to commit suicide by jumping off the bridge into the River Miljacker, only to find that the water was only two feet deep! He was arrested but later made a national hero by the Bosnians.

Resuming our exploration we came across a woman, making and displaying her beautiful curtains.

In our wanderings we found ourselves outside Sarajevo's largest mosque, the Begova Guena, which is actually the third largest in Europe. A high stone wall surrounded the place, but we were able to see into the courtyard through iron-railed apertures. Before entering the mosque, people must first remove their footwear and wash their feet in the fountain outside. And five times a day services are held!

As we wended our way back to our hotel, we saw dreamy old Moslem priests with turbaned fez and tight fitting black breeches, and heavily veiled women in their all-enshrouding grey or mauve costumes. All this contrasted with dignified men clothed in smart suits, and young beauties in the latest western fashions, with mere wisps of veils.

Passing a little shop where the proprietor was busy making fezes, the temptation proved too great for some of the party, and he derived much pleasure in fitting each head.

Back at the hotel we enjoyed a good meal, before securing our cycles to resume our journey. John and Fred were leaving us here to ride on to Belgrade, from where they were to enter Romania and later Bulgaria.

By three o'clock we were riding back through the west end of the town we had entered twenty-four hours previously. And so we left Sarajevo, said to be more Turkish than any Turkish city.

After twenty easy miles we rejoined our original route and turned away south-west, with great pine-clad hills on either side and a winding stream which kept pace with us. But soon our road took an upward tilt and we climbed a small pass. I say 'small'; actually we climbed to over 3,000 feet, but the going was not hard. By the roadside we noticed many gravestones, possibly indicating where men had been killed in battle.

We had tea at a wayside inn, and here were served tea with lemon, after the Russian style. No milk, of course; the only time we did see milk was in the larger hotels.

It was pitch dark when we commenced the descent of the Ivan Pass. But no ordinary darkness this – it was just as if a great black cloth had been draped over our heads, blotting out almost everything. Gingerly we descended, brakes hard on and eyes straining to keep the edge of the precipice within the range of our feeble battery lamps. Then there was sudden excitement as Fred came tearing through the party and disappeared into the darkness ahead. Came a grating noise and a clatter, then silence. Had Fred gone over the edge?

Happily, it wasn't as bad as that. Apparently, his rear brake cable had given in under the strain, and as his front had been damaged on the railway, he was left without any means of stopping. When he found himself rapidly gaining speed, he had abandoned his cycle by leaping off.

We mended his brake cable and continued. It was then that we were able to follow the progress, far away across the valley, of a train assisted by three engines, each belching a beautiful fountain of red sparks into the blackness of the night. Owing to the absence of coal in the country these engines burn wood, and in consequence at night-time, come the showers of sparks.

We slept the night at a little inn at Konjic, though the sleeping part of the procedure did not commence until well after midnight owing to the pandemonium which filled the village. This inn was equipped with radio, and a speaker of the most valuable type was fixed outside the doorway, and emitting a mighty blare of dance music. Now, opposite to our inn was a little coffee shop, which to our amazement possessed a brass band of six persons, despite the fact that the premises would hold no more than a dozen customers. Well, the band crashed and boomed and a female with a particularly shrill voice shrieked the choruses. This in competition with the radio created a veritable hell – all so surprising in this peaceful country.

But Konjic let us off lightly as we were only asked for 1s. 8d. each for our supper, bed and breakfast. Konjic, we learned, was the stopping place for the train bound from the coast to Sarajevo, and should anyone require lunch, arrangements were made for the train to be delayed while the person dined at the inn. Such was Yugoslavia. What provided our most pleasing memory of Konjic was without doubt the fine, six-arch bridge over the River Neretva, which was reflected in the calm water.

Following the river we enjoyed good wheeling for many miles. We passed the most primitive church ever: a wooden shed with, nearby, a belfry composed of lengths of wood, surmounted by a cross.

Then we entered a great gorge, with massive grey crags rising high overhead, while below boiled the greenish waters of the river. Hardly a trace of vegetation was visible – nothing but the grey rocks and the pale green river, while green and brown lizards darted away from our grinding wheels.

We proceeded and the sun rose high in the sky until it beat down on us pitilessly. Every minute it seemed to be getting hotter and hotter, and whenever we got off our cycles to take photographs, the dreadful heat rose up around us. Bernard Newman had warned us not to go in August, because of the heat, but in our case, with holiday dates fixed by various circumstances, we hadn't much option.

We rode through a tunnel, delightfully cool after the sweltering heat outside, and we passed a horse and cart with the driver stretched out, full length, asleep. Even the horse was asleep!

Gorge – Konjik to Mostar.

The Bosnian family who fed us when 'starving'.

We were becoming ravenously hungry, but the hamlet we were watching for had apparently disappeared since our maps were printed, as we saw no sign of any habitation. Hundreds of feet above us, slowly circling over the crags, we saw, like mere specks, a couple of eagles. We had heard of eagles in these parts with a wing-span of eight feet, and capable of carrying off a sheep.

We came upon several landslides – thousands of tons of rock and earth which had avalanched down the mountainside and over the road. No

Accident.

attempt had been made to dig the road out – they had merely placed a crude wooden rail over the obstruction, and called that the road!

Hunger was now becoming a serious matter and, to make things worse, a gale of wind blew. But no ordinary wind this, as we had experienced before; it must have been heated by a furnace. Eventually we came upon a little white-washed house before which the family was seated round a table, presumably resting from their labours. They gave us black bread and big juicy tomatoes, while a youngster was despatched for a pail of water. If that could be classed as a meal, it was one I enjoyed more than any other!

The gale was by now more violent than ever when we took to the road once more. It was in fact difficult to make any progress against it at all.

The old bridge at Mostar.

Eventually we reached a little village, called Livac and here found crowds of people from the nearby town of Mostar. It appeared to be some sort of holiday, with everyone in their Sunday best! The girls were dressed in white costumes with brightly coloured aprons and headkerchiefs, while the men wore white trousers and shirts, with coloured sashes.

Half a mile beyond the village we ran into trouble – or rather trouble ran into us. Five youths on cycles approached, presumably from Mostar, and with the gale of wind behind, were making full use of the elements. Riding abreast, they were using the full width of the road. One fellow came tearing straight at me, on his extreme off-side of the road and he just smacked 'bang-slap' into me.

I knew my collar bone was in trouble but, having rectified a few problems with the bike, we were able to continue as far as Mostar, and here got fixed up for the night at the Hercegovina Hotel. We had just finished our evening meal, at a table outside the hotel, when suddenly, terrific excitement broke out. Waiters rushed out and commenced grabbing tablecloths and chairs and swirling them inside, while we were bustled inside along with everyone else. As if by magic, the street became deserted. What on earth was happening?

Then the wind, which by this time was howling through the streets, suddenly brought with it clouds of sand and dust, and everything was obliterated by a raging sand-storm. Trees were bent under the stress, while pieces of paper and other debris were swept away into the fog of sand. After a while torrential rain flooded down, and the wind died completely. Blinding flares of lightning flashed almost incessantly, and thunder rolled and groaned away overhead.

When the rain had eased off we strolled off through the town to see what Mostar had to offer, and found our way to the bridge for which the town was famous. Of Turkish origin, the bridge was a single arch structure crossing the River Neretva, flowing sixty feet beneath the highest point of the arch.

Mostar was quite a large town, as we found next morning, and the river offered us plenty of subjects for the cameras. We could always include a white minaret in our pictures.

The Moslem women, we found, wore rather different costumes here. Some we saw were clothed in a heavy, dark blue robe, from head to feet, while a veil was dropped from immediately below the eyes, with a black cloth across the forehead, leaving a narrow slit for the eyes.

As we left Mostar, and made our attack on the rocky mountains of the Karst, we saw, growing by the roadside, such fruits as pomegranates, figs, melons, oranges and lemons.

We were now entering Dalmatia and the heat was even greater than before as we neared the coast, while the fact that we had to climb a pass didn't ease the situation.

On the far side of this pass we found the valley laid out in a wonderful patchwork of tiny green plots of cultivated land. We saw rivers and streams which, after winding their way through a valley for miles, suddenly disappeared underground. We saw little blue lakes, like mere pools in the rocky waste. Further on we rode past tobacco fields, while outside the peasants' cottages we saw tobacco leaves hung drying.

At the next village, Siroki Brijeg, we found a miniature industrial centre. We approached the village inn for food, and on learning that we were English, one of the locals was despatched to fetch the village interpreter. This turned out to be a delightful chap who had, he told us, spent many years in Chicago. He told us that his village had grown, in ten years, from a mere hamlet into a place the size of a town, directly in consequence of the aluminium quarries in the neighbourhood. He told us how the Croats badly wanted their liberty from the Serbians. Yugoslavia was, of course, created after the Great War from parts of Austria, and the whole of Bosnia-Hercegovina, Serbia and Montenegro.

The Croats then talked incessantly of 'when the war comes', but as we know, they had to wait fifty years! Sayavanja Ilija was quite enthusiastic about the war they were planning when, he said, the British would help them. 'We want Britain to accept three ports on the Adriatic, Split, Sibenik and Kortor,' he said.

On the road once more, the approach of another thunderstorm decided us to get a move on. A pass lay ahead and we were anxious to be over the top before the storm burst.

Never, now, did we see water trickling by the roadside, and when we asked for water at the village at the top of the pass, a key had to be obtained and a well opened especially for us.

As we swept, by mighty hairpin bends, down into Imotski, we saw ahead of us the fierce peaks of the Dinaric Alps glowing red in the light of the setting sun.

Over a snack we had an interesting conversation with El Capitan, as he was introduced to us. He told us that he was Italian although he had a house in Imotski. He had several times visited Hull in his ship, he told us. We were introduced to the local maestro, who flashed a gold-toothed grin at us. Although he offered to play us some music at a later hour, when the time came I'm afraid our maestro was somewhat under the influence, and beyond an occasional sloppy grin he did nothing to entertain us.

El Capitan took us to see what he described as the Black Sea. This turned out to be a remarkable hole in the ground which was like the crater of some extinct volcano. The hole was several hundred yards across and the bottom, 600 feet below, was full of inky black water. Then we were shown a large depression in the ground, the result we understood, of a land subsidence.

We were fascinated to see a young girl carrying a barrel of water on her back. How did she get such a heavy load up there? Well, she merely looped the two ropes around the barrel, brought the two ends over her shoulders – and yanked it up!

For the cost of 7d. each we obtained a good lunch of soup, spaghetti, cheese, bread and melon, and then onward towards the Adriatic, which lay beyond a range of mountains ahead.

At Blato, my cycling, for this tour at any rate, came to an end. My cycle slipped sideways in dismounting and, momentarily forgetting my wonky shoulder, I tried to yank it upright. Whether my collar bone was already broken or not, I don't know, but this certainly finished it off. My arm was now quite useless, and although I tried to ride with one hand on the bars, this proved to be impossible, owing to the rough nature of the road. So Pip tied it up, and we commenced to walk.

The others having gone on ahead, it was agreed that Pip should chase after them and then continue to Split, where it might be possible to find some conveyance to return to rescue me. We had twenty-five miles to do to Split and the time was 3 p.m. when Fred and I commenced walking.

By five o'clock we had covered about five miles and hadn't seen a living soul as we tramped on into the wilderness. There was nothing but the bare mountains and the road, dusty and stony, winding on into the distance. By six o'clock we were more than hungry; we were ravenous, so when a cottage came into view we welcomed the sight. We were given rings of bread – as hard as concrete – and a jug of red wine. We soaked the bread in the wine before we could eat it. Veritably iron rations!

We came to a mighty pass and slowly wended our way up the great loops, resting on each bend. Fred's poor old feet were complaining about walking in his comparatively light cycling shoes, on such abominable roads, and in such heat.

By now it was dark, but when we came to the summit, the scene which opened out before us, almost made us forget our troubles. The great black bulk of the mountains slid down into the inky waters of the Adriatic, while across the water gleamed the great yellow sphere of the moon.

Further on – joy of joy – a car approached. 'Good,' we thought, 'The lads have managed it.' The lights on the car grew nearer and I flashed my cycle lamp to indicate our presence. When about twenty yards away, the car stopped and we moved forward to greet whoever had come to rescue us, but then to our amazement the car came back to life, rushed past us and disappeared into the distance, leaving us standing! Somebody probably had a bad shock, and to this day, thinks he was being held up by bandits!

At nine o'clock we came to a village and halted to drink at a wayside fountain, while great dogs bounded out from among the buildings, barking fearfully, and suspicious eyes scrutinised us from doors opened a few inches.

Fred's feet were really giving him problems, and when we had been walking for nearly seven hours he said he could go no further. So we collected branches from some nearby cypress trees to make a bed, and prepared to sleep for a few hours.

But then we heard the sound of an approaching motor vehicle, heading in the same direction as ourselves. I never thought I'd live to see the day that I would welcome the approach of a motor car, but it was so. Standing in the middle of the road with our cycle lamps we persuaded the driver to stop. The vehicle turned out to be a bus heading for the same destination as us, Split. With the help of an Italian, a passenger on the bus, we made known our problems, and soon our cycles were stowed away on the roof and we were seated comfortably, as we thought, inside.

With a jolt we set off, and immediately I wished they had left me on the roadside to die in peace. The road was full of pot-holes – indeed, pot-holes doesn't describe them; they were craters – and the bus bumped, jolted and lurched along at a speed unbelievable on such a road, while I tried, unsuccessfully, to hold my shoulder against the jolts. We rattled and bashed over a pass, and went skating down the far side on a road which was a mere ledge on the mountainside.

It was 11.30 p.m. when we reached Split, and the bus driver, having disposed of his passengers, very kindly took me round to the hospital, where I learned what I already knew, that my collar bone was broken. I refused to stay the night in the hospital, and the bus driver, who had stayed with us, then took us to the Central Hotel where we settled in for the night.

We were served with dinner at a table outside the hotel at midnight, and despite the fact that we were the only guests present, a full orchestra played for us, a Union Jack was placed on the table, and a waiter cut up my food! In the morning I went round to the hospital again to get my shoulder tied up while Fred set off to find the rest of the party. You see I had the money for all of us. Our efforts to find the others failed, but we did run across our Italian friend of the previous night. Some mystery appeared to surround this chap, for despite the fact that he carried an Italian passport, he told us that he was English. His name was Antonio Amato.

He told us that he was in charge of a party of British soldiers on board HMS *Hampshire*, a British warship anchored in the bay. He said that he had left the ship at Dubrovnik for a few days' holiday, and intended rejoining her at Fiume. He was obviously an officer of some standing, and he offered to take me across to the warships so that the ship's doctor could have a look at my shoulder. Like an idiot, I refused, and have ever since regretted not taking advantage of such an opportunity. Anyhow, whoever he was, we got on with him very well.

Split is really a wonderful old place. A quarter of the town is built within the walls of an old Diocletian palace, covering ten acres. Shops, houses, hotels are all built there, in many instances leaning on the walls of the palace. One quite amazing feature of Split was the remarkable shops built onto the end of small ships anchored against the harbour wall. Under canvas awnings, fruit, vegetables and merchandise were offered for sale. As the ships rose and fell with the movement of the water, it was a miracle how the piled-up fruit remained in position!

Fred and Antonio visited the beach for a swim, but, of course, I was denied this experience.

We eventually ran across the rest of the party at about 4 p.m. and it appeared that they had been searching for us as we for them.

When Fred and I came to settle up at our hotel we were only charged 6s. for dinner, bed and breakfast. No wonder this was a favourite haunt of the Duke and Duchess of Windsor!

Filling in the time before our train departed, we spent some time sipping drinks at an outside cafe on the harbour front, when suddenly all the town's lights went out, to the accompaniment of shrieks from the promenading females. It was significant that when the lights went out, a waiter came out and posted himself alongside our table!

Wandering back towards the station we were amazed to see a railway porter ride by on an English touring cycle. It was Fred's. He recognised it, let out a yell of rage, and set off in pursuit.

When we arrived back at the station, one of the now customary thunderstorms broke, and Pip had a shot at getting a record of a flash of lightning. He was lucky and got a beauty. You can visualise how spectacular these storms are when I tell you that streaks of lightning are blazing down all round the horizon, while thunder rolls almost incessantly.

By strenuous effort we secured a compartment to ourselves, and soon we were jolting and rattling into the night. And then home via Zagreb, Munich, Antwerp and Harwich.

So came to an end a truly amazing holiday. During the fifteen days, we had travelled almost 4,000 miles (400 of them by cycle); we had suffered some inconveniences and discomfort, but considered we had been amply rewarded by what we had seen and experienced in that country I have described as Europe's Orient.

The total cost of the tour was £16, fifty per cent of which was accounted for by steamer and train fares!

Some Special Memories

An Easter Weekend in the Lakes – 1930

At 6.45 a.m. I left home for a four day run round the Lakes and Yorkshire Dales in weather that was inclined to be showery and against a north to north-west wind that was rather more than strong. The seven miles to Beverley occupied nearly forty-five minutes and I began to realise that I was in for a pretty stiff ride. However, I settled down to it and got along steadily over the Wolds to Market Weighton and across the Plain of York; just before reaching York I saw a perfect rainbow. I rode into York at 9.45 a.m. and left by Blossom Street over more flat uninteresting roads to Wetherby. I had intended making my way from York through Tollerton, West Tanfield and Masham through Wensleydale and Garsdale to Sedbergh and Kendal but as this would have meant a direct head wind I changed my course at York for Wharfedale. As the church clock struck 11 a.m. I was riding over the bridge out of Wetherby and into Lower Wharfedale. It had by this time turned out quite bright and I proceeded onward through Harewood and Pool to Otley. It was now about mid-day and I was hitting the full force of the Harrogate, Bradford and Leeds motor coaches and cars. Still, after passing through Burley and Ilkley I avoided most of the traffic at Addingham by taking the direct road to Skipton instead of going round by Bolton Bridge. Shortly before Draughton and just past the Reservoir I partook of lunch, having covered 76 miles.

This very important business occupied from 1.10 p.m. to 1.45 p.m. and then I remounted my iron steed and free-wheeled down into Skipton where I was favoured by a huge slice of luck. In the centre of this town I took a wrong turning and journeyed half a mile along the Clitheroe road before I realised my mistake. However, having returned to Skipton I ran across a laddie from Huddersfield, who like myself was heading for the Lakes so we joined forces and pedalled onward. Had I not taken the wrong road I should have had the weekend on my own and I am sure I should not have had quite such an enjoyable time. Cyril Garner was the Hon. Secretary of the Huddersfield Road Club, and whilst he was a first class twelve and twenty-four hour time trial specialist, he was also a keen tourist with the same fondness for 'rough stuff' that I had.

Riding easily we soon left Gargrave and Long Preston behind and passed through Settle and then climbed up to 815 feet over Giggleswick Scar, following this by a long drop and an undulating ride through Clapham and Ingleton to Kirby Lonsdale, where, by the Devil's Bridge over the River Lune, we fed. We spent forty-five minutes over our tea, during the course of which we amused ourselves by feeding a robin on bread crumbs, and then we passed out of Kirby Lonsdale at 5.30 p.m. and another thirteen miles of more or less easy going brought us to Kendal which we left by the Windermere road, reaching this latter place at 7.30 p.m.

We then free-wheeled down to Bowness Pier and after admiring Lake Windermere and its wooded banks for ten minutes, set our wheels northward for Ambleside. About a mile short of Ambleside we turned west for Elterwater and Langdale – our destination for the day. The magnificent view of the Langdale Pikes silhouetted against the setting sun, with the clear waters of Windermere in the foreground, is one I shall never forget. The weather had completely changed and the evening could not have been more perfect.

At 8.45 p.m. we could have been seen pedalling joyously into Langdale village and following a hunt round were soon tucking into an enormous supper at Walthwaite Farm. As the sleeping accommodation was full up here we were to spend the night at another house at the other side of the village, but you can well imagine our surprise when on going outside with the gentleman who was to guide us to our beds we found a prehistoric Morris car awaiting us. So after cycling 143 miles we were destined to finish the day with a half mile jaunt in a motor car of all things on earth. Having climbed in, in the approved style, the searchlights were switched on and we slid down the hill towards a stone wall facing the end of the road. The wall got nearer and I got hold of the door handle in readiness. However, we swung round a corner and I breathed again. A few more seconds and our motor ride was over and a quarter of an hour later we were sleeping the sleep of the just. Three clocks in the village struck every half hour and we awoke every half hour for the first couple of hours, but after that the clocks either struck no more or we had become acclimatised; anyhow we slept on until 7 a.m.

A scrumptious breakfast having gone the way of all good breakfasts when cyclists are about, we mounted our irons at 9.15 a.m. and sallied forth into the gale which had risen by this time. Riding back to Elterwater we climbed over the hill to Little Langdale Tarn and then on to the foot of Wrynose Pass where we dismounted and walked onward and upward to the summit (1070 feet) and photographed the Three Shires Stone at the spot where Lancashire, Cumberland and Westmorland meet. The visibility was not so good as it had been the night before; still, we had a fine view back down the pass, of the road winding and twisting its way through the valley. The weather was also inclined to be showery but we found capes were only a handicap as it was impossible to keep them down, so we decided that it would be better to let the wind dry us after each shower. It did this all right as it was blowing at about 50 miles per hour. The gale was at our backs and we enjoyed a rapid dash down to Cockley Beck, every hundred yards or so splashing through a watersplash. From Cockley Beck we commenced the ascent of Hardknott Pass the summit of which we reached after a good climb and then from about 1,300 feet we started the steep descent into Eskdale. On one particularly steep bit I discovered that with my rims being wet my brakes were not holding and that I could not stop if I wanted to. My speed increased slowly to 12 m.p.h. and I came to the conclusion that something ought to be done about it. Directly in front the road swung round to the right with a sheer drop over the edge straight on and I was faced with either attempting to ride down to the bottom of the pass and risk taking the corners, or falling off at once. So I got off. Putting my left foot on to the road I trailed it a few yards before catching it against one of the rocks with which the road was strewn and followed this by a very successful attempt at looping the loop.

Having ascertained that my bike was none the worse we continued on foot down this section before remounting. Reaching a road we simply flew over the next mile (wind assisted) to the Woolpack Inn which we had decided on for lunch. We arrived at just 12 o'clock noon. Lunch over at 1.30 p.m. we rode a further mile along the Eskdale Road to Boot where we turned off north for the Burn Moor Pass to Wasdale Head. Then, soon after leaving Boot, we came across a charming little water wheel and before pushing onward photographed this.

Out on the open moor the fun began. The wind was by now, to say the least of it, terrific and every few minutes we could see a hail storm approaching over the mountain tops and then, before we had covered many yards, we would be in the centre of a furious blizzard which absolutely numbed faces and hands although the latter were protected by gloves. Our capes were useless as had we dared to take them out they would have been torn to ribbons by the wind. As soon as we saw these blizzards appear over the mountains we made a rush for the nearest boulder or wall and stopped there until it was over. After struggling on for about two miles the track fizzled out and we were left to find our own path over the heather and rock. We passed the Tarn, the surface of which was like a boiling cauldron, and soon afterwards sighted Wasdale Head.

At 4.45 p.m. we staggered into this tiny village for tea. Wast Water was covered by foam topped waves while over the surface hung a curtain of swirling spray. Tea finished and feeling fit again for anything, we moved off at 5.45 p.m. to cross over Sty Head Pass between Great Gable (2,949 feet) and Scafell Pike (3,210) to Seathwaite. Many walkers had given up the idea of doing this pass that day on account of the terrific wind which was blowing straight down the pass. The going was quite easy to commence with and we were beginning to think that our task was not going to be so difficult as we expected especially as we could see distinctly the track over the mountains. However, the further we progressed the more difficult became the going. The path climbed more steeply and the surface rougher and our pace, like the conditions, deteriorated.

After pushing forward for some time we reached the 'Struggle' where the gradient became something like 1 in 1 and the track just a mass of loose stones and rock. Owing to the wind it was impossible to shoulder our bikes, as had we done so we should have been blown down the pass. So we had to scramble on, sliding and stumbling among loose stones. I was ten minutes on one spot until I found a firm part of the track. Having struggled up the 'Struggle' the gradient eased somewhat though the track deteriorated more than ever. We now had to clamber over rocks – sometimes stumbling along up a stream, which in places formed the path, sometimes lifting our bikes on to rocks which barred our way and climbing up afterwards, and sometimes climbing up first and hoisting the bikes after us. Nearing the top we had to cross the stream by a plank bridge and to accomplish this we had to edge our way across half a step at a time, as had we been caught off our balance by the wind we should have most probably finished up among the rocks.

We eventually passed the Tarn and the track leading off over Esk Hause and commenced the downward trek. This turned out to be more rapid though still a tricky game. In places we lifted up our bikes and jumped from crag to crag and at other times we ran down the track at about evens taking enormous strides. In this way we soon reached Seathwaite and a road along which we rode into Seatoller where accommodation was found after three unsuccessful attempts. We arrived at 8.30 p.m. the ascent of Sty Head having taken 1 hour 30 minutes and the descent to Seatoller 1 hour 15 minutes. A good wash and a scrumptious hot supper concluded a day of glorious adventure. The mileage for the day was only 24 though in that 24 miles was crammed more incidents than any double century of ordinary riding.

Sunday morning brought a big change in the weather. The wind had moderated and the sun was shining, so, breakfast over and having fitted new brake blocks, we moved off at 9.45 a.m. heading northward for Keswick on roads which seemed like velvet after our previous day's experience. Borrowdale was looking glorious in the sunshine and, feeling surprisingly fit instead of stiff and bruised as we had expected, we got along nicely past the Bowder Stone and alongside beautiful Derwent Water and into Keswick where half an hour was spent whilst I got my front brake repaired and the Huddersfield Laddie went in search of a film for his camera.

We got clear of Keswick by 11 a.m. and were soon riding alongside splendid Thirlmere with Helvellyn, whose peaks, like the other mountains, were liberally coated with snow, on our left. Leaving Thirlmere behind we climbed to the summit of Dunmail, almost before we realized we were climbing, and then followed a glorious rush downhill to Grasmere. A few miles further along we had a picnic lunch by the banks of Rydal Water before continuing into Ambleside. From Ambleside we proceeded on foot up the Kirkstone road by Stock Gill, climbing from about 100 feet at Ambleside to 1,476 feet at the Travellers Rest Inn at the top of the pass in about three miles. A short halt was made at the summit whilst I photographed the inn and then, on our saddles once more, we shot downwards at about 40 m.p.h. towards pretty little Brothers Water nestling among the hills at the foot of the pass. With Brothers Water and the little village of Patterdale behind us we commenced the fine ride along the shore of Ullswater.

As we rode onward, admiring the beautiful mountain and Lake scenery, we marvelled at those remarkable stone walls marching over the landscape – no matter how high the altitude nor how steep the gradient. Who built them and how? We noticed them particularly while passing over Sty Head, running straight up almost perpendicular faces. The miles slid by among this glorious scenery and in a very short time Ullswater was behind us and we were crossing Pooley Bridge and another four miles further at Brougham we left the Penrith road and turned our wheels in the direction of Appleby and the snow covered moors of Yorkshire which were now clearly visible on the horizon.

About eleven miles of rather less attractive country but over a very pleasant undulating road and Appleby was reached and a good tea put us in great form for the evening ride through Kirkby Stephen and over Birkdale Common to Swaledale. Leaving Appleby we kept up a steady pace and soon reached Kirkby Stephen and a mile and a half further on along the Hawes road turned off on to the Birkdale road and immediately commenced climbing steadily. Riding and walking for two miles and we were at the summit, just under 1,700 feet, and covered by six inches of snow. We paused to gaze back at the magnificent panorama laid out before us, with the church and houses of Kirkby Stephen standing black against the setting sun, whilst the whole of the Vale was lying beneath a golden haze and in the background our last glimpse of the Lakeland Peaks. Then eastward once more, five miles of rapid riding on a falling gradient brought us to Keld where Kirkdale Beck joins Stonesdale Beck and continues as the River Swale on its journey down to the sea. Passing on through Thwaite we were soon at Muker where the Huddersfield Laddie had arranged to meet some friends. Yes! as we dashed downhill we saw them standing in the roadway so after exchanging addresses I continued on my way alone towards Gunnerside and two miles from this village I met Syd, on foot, coming to meet me. Together we walked the aforesaid two miles into Gunnerside when, after a bit of a wait, we had supper at Mrs Davidson's. Our bed was at another cottage and having stumbled through the pitch black village we retired to rest after a really fine day which had been free from rain. A thoroughly enjoyable day's wheeling. Mileage 84.

Breakfast over, we rode away under an overcast sky and passing over the bridge headed up the dale for a mile before turning southward for Askrigg by the Summer Lodge Pass. Walking and riding, after a couple of miles we reached the snow belt and continued towards Wensleydale over the snow covered moors. At times the whiteness covered the road to a depth of nine inches. Before dropping down into Askrigg we were favoured by a very fine view of Semer Water set among the moors at the far side of Wensleydale. With brakes hard on we slithered down into Askrigg and set our wheels eastward for Aysgarth where we went in search of the falls. In these we were disappointed so without further delay we headed into Bishop Dale pedalling through pleasant scenery before ascending Kidstones Hill from where we dashed down into Wharfedale, breaking our freewheel at Cray to photograph the waterfalls over which plenty of water was flowing. We intended having lunch at Buckden but when we arrived it was to find the place in the hands of motorists so we naturally carried on in search of some quieter spot. This we found, after riding easily through Starbotton and Kettlewell, at the Anglers Arms at Kilnsey.

Arriving at 1 p.m. we spent the next hour and a quarter in demolishing lunch and then with the road sliding away beneath our wheels once more we crossed the Wharfe at Coniston and continued along the east bank as far as Grassington where we left the Wharfe and headed across the Appletreewick Moors to Pateley Bridge. Near Hebden we witnessed a hawk making a kill. It hung stationary about thirty or forty feet above the ground for several seconds and then dropped to the grass like a stone and immediately commenced devouring some poor unfortunate animal or bird.

Near Stump Cross Caverns I smashed my derailleur cable, though, as it had done 6,000 miles, I suppose I can't grumble. Anyhow I became a single gear merchant for the rest of the day. Following the tricky descent of Greenhow Hill, we climbed up Pateley's cobbled main street and out on to the Knaresborough road and, after a rather uneventful ride along roads which, considering it was a bank holiday, were very quiet, we reached Ripley. From here a steady ride through Knaresborough and Green Hammerton brought us to York at 6 p.m. with an enormous appetite for tea. Having let our appetites run their course at the Windmill Inn we tackled the last stretch for home. The weather had turned out simply glorious by now and with the tramlines of York behind us we were soon watching the milestones sail by until Market Weighton hove into sight. Market Weighton hill offered no resistance whatever and before we realised it we were flashing over the undulations to Bishop Burton, where we paused to light up. After leaving Syd in Beverley I became overcome by an intense feeling of fitness and could not help 'standing on them' for the remaining seven miles home which I reached at 9.50 p.m.

Four days of glorious life.

The Trough of Bowland – August 1930

At 11.15 p.m. Eric, Ken, Percy and myself moved off from Inglemire Bridge under a beautiful starlit sky with the moon just sinking over the horizon on a run round the northern part of Lancashire and the Yorkshire Dales. With only a slight southern wind blowing we very soon left Beverley behind and then travelled over the pleasant undulations to Market Weighton. Then there were nineteen flat miles to York, this ancient city, which must be passed through on all trips to the Dale. Another thirteen miles of flat and a first halt was made at Wetherby for necessary refuelling of lamps and bodies. Forty-five minutes later and we were off once more with the happy thought that the fifty miles of rather uninteresting country which we were always compelled to cover before thrusting into the Pennines were behind us. Continuing through the silent streets of Wetherby over the bridge we turned right along the Otley road and with the sky already lightening swung along at a steady 14 m.p.h. through Collingham, and up on to Harewood Bank. One by one we doused our lights as we sped along between the lime trees.

Reaching Harewood village we dashed madly down the hill and on through Arthington, Pool, Otley, Burley, Ilkley, Addingham and up the two mile climb to the Draughton Reservoir and here paused to gaze in admiration at the magnificent picture. The sun had by this time risen over Blubberhouses Moor and was shining across the still waters of the reservoir. As we stood there breathing the cool morning air I thought how everything – the hills and the mountains, the roads, the little villages and even the dirty industrial towns – are cleansed and purified during the hours of darkness and prepared to commence each day clean and wholesome. A further snack was partaken of here, and then awheel again, we freewheeled down through Draughton Village and on into Skipton. Here taking the Clitheroe road, we pedalled onward through charming well tree'd country passing Broughton, East Marton and West Marton to Gisburn. On the bridge, over the Leeds–Liverpool Canal at East Marton we dismounted to watch a barge being drawn along the canal by a horse on the towing path. Beneath us we noticed a milestone on the canal bank – Leeds 36½ miles. The horse plodded along steadily and rounding a bend both the horse and barge were hidden from our view although the hardworking animal could still be heard persistently plodding onward. The waters smoothed over once more and we remounted and continued over the pleasant undulating road to Gisburn.

At Gisburn we branched off to the right and rode through the most delightful lanes it would be possible to find anywhere, through Gisburn Park, over the River Ribble, a steady climb, and then down into Bolton by Bowland, a most charming little spot which I had long wished to visit. Although Bolton by Bowland couldn't provide us with breakfast we obtained this at Holden, half a mile further on. Feeling very much refreshed by a wash and a good breakfast and Eric having unsuccessfully endeavoured to find a puncture in his tyre we rode onward at about 10 a.m. We gathered from the hundreds of cyclists streaming through the village that there was a meet somewhere in the neighbourhood.

It was at Bowland that we met up with Eddie Rayner and George Munson who had left home earlier than us and had arrived at Bowland the night before. If my memory serves me correctly it was later on this particular run that Eddie had the misfortune to sustain severe gear trouble. Not long a member of our group, Eddie was riding a peculiar cycle (was it a Triumph?) fitted with a variable gear housed in the chainwheel. Now this gear was provided with many thousands of ball bearings which unfortunately became spread widely along the road. Incredibly enough we managed to put Eddie's cycle together again and proceed.

The sun had by now warmed up the atmosphere pretty well and pullovers etc. were stowed away before passing down the lane to Sawley, where there are the remains of an abbey, and then along the main road, now very much alive with petrol vehicles, through Chatburn and on into Clitheroe. Having rattled our way over the setts we turned right along quieter roads to Low Moor where Ken took his turn at puncture mending. Eric's tyre, by the way, was still hard so his deflation will have to go down as one of the mystery tyre subsidences which had been so plentiful that year.

We had crossed the county boundary from West Yorkshire into Lancashire near Sawley and we now returned into Yorkshire and climbed steadily for some distance until we reached a fork in the road. The left hand fork, the signpost told us, would take us by the main road to Whiteley, while the right hand road, which went straight up a steep hill with a rotten surface, was the old road to Whiteley. We naturally took the old, steep and rotten road, and slogged up to the top of the hill and then down with brakes hard on, bumping all over the road down into Whiteley.

But what a view met our eyes as we topped the brow of the hill. Below was the pretty village of Whiteley, set in a beautiful valley with the finely wooded slopes curving down from the high fells on either side while through the valley trickled the winding river Hodder. We rode on through this glorious valley which reminded us so much of one of the Lakeland Dales, along by the river which we several times crossed, through the collection of farmhouses which forms Dunsop Bridge village and, following more climbing, the hills closed in on us and we dropped down into the Trough of Bowland, or as it is known locally – the Trough of Bolland. As the name implies this is just like a huge trough sunk into the moors. We crossed over into Lancashire once more and rode along shut in on all sides by the huge hills. No wonder it is so popular with the campers.

As we expected, a steep climb was necessary to get out of the 'trough' with a gradient of about 1 in 7. Still, we all managed it without dismounting, and having found a tree sheltered spot by the riverside halted for lunch. Lunch over and Percy having smoked his cigarette, we freewheeled onward for a few miles until another long climb brought us to the top of Abbeystead Fell at 940 feet. What would have been a glorious view across the Morecambe Bay was rather spoiled by the heat haze.

Still, the mouth of the River Lune and, further to the right, the observatory at Lancaster were visible. Now followed an ultra rapid freewheel for about three miles down to the Conder River. Ken and I were tearing along side by side when about halfway down something flew off his bike, struck the road in front of me and ricocheted over the stone wall which bounded the road. A little later on, when desiring to put on his front brake, he was surprised to find that nothing happened in response to pressing the lever. The something which had come off his bike was a brake block and shoe. Hereafter all steep hills had to be walked down.

From Conder River another short climb and we dropped down into Lancaster. Before descending each hill in this district you were confronted by a board informing you that the hill was dangerous and that fatal accidents had occurred. Crossing the canal in the town we turned right and rode north-east along an easy road for Ingleton. Passing Caton and Hornby Castle, we continued through Melling and Burton in Lonsdale to Ingleton where, as it was nearly five o'clock, we had tea and then headed for Dentdale. Turning northward at Thornton in Lonsdale we climbed like fury for a couple of miles, and then for the next three miles the gradient was easy as we rode alongside the Kingsdale Beck between Greygarth Hill and Whernside. Leaving Kingsdale House at 994 feet the road developed into a grass track and ran upward alongside a wood and continued climbing steadily to the summit at White Shaw Moss at over 1,500 feet.

Here a most magnificent view was laid out before us. The road fell sheer away in front of us into Deepdale with Crag Hill heaped up on the left and the great mass of Whernside on the right. The varying shades of green on the steep hillsides were just touched by the last rays of the setting sun, whilst a thousand or more feet below us was set out a beautiful patchwork of miniature fields, woods and scattered farmhouses and about three miles ahead Rise Hill rose up out of Dentdale into which Deepdale opened out. This view alone would be worth riding three hundred miles on stone setts, uphill and against a 50 mile per hour wind between rows of Council houses.

We commenced the precipitous descent. For some distance we kept to our saddles (except Ken) until the time came when the road swung round and appeared to drop sheer down, then coming back on its tracks to form, as Kuklos puts it, a huge U. Kuklos had said that this drop terrified him and it certainly fetched us out of the saddle and made us walk down very cautiously. Reaching a rideable road once more we dashed forward down the dale until the sound of rushing water brought us off our bikes to discover a very fine waterfall hidden away in a little glen. A few minutes later we arrived at Holly Bush where our request for accommodation for the night was successful. This turned out to be the spot favoured by Kuklos when in the district. Supper over and after Eric had had a few minutes on the piano we made our last climb of the day – upstairs to bed. Thirty seconds later we were sleeping the sleep of the cyclist who has ridden nearly a century during the hours he should have been sleeping the night before. I awoke next morning to hear the delightful spattering of rain on the windows and we gazed out at the glistening trees and the low clouds slowly moving across the face of Whernside opposite. Having breakfasted and Percy having mended a puncture we made a start at about 10.30 a.m. It was not raining so very much now so we moved off without the handicap of capes.

We rode out into glorious Dentdale (the finest dale in Yorkshire) and through the quaint old world village of Dent with its queer, narrow cobbled streets and on towards Sedbergh. Numerous streams were dashing down from the heights of Long Bank and Black Hill. Although it was such a dull and, in other surroundings, possibly miserable morning, the weather could not deaden the beauties of this glorious dale. We were sorry indeed when the end of the dale was reached and left behind; still further delights were in store for us after passing through Sedbergh where we turned our wheels eastward and aided by a stiff breeze rode onward into Garsdale, which if not up to the standard of Dentdale was certainly very fine. Rising steadily we passed between Baugh Fell and Rise Hill, on the other side of which we had earlier in the morning ridden through in Dentdale, by the tiny village of Garsdale and up to Garsdale Head. Then a few minutes later we reached the Moorcock Inn at the junction of the Kirkby Stephen road. It had been raining steadily all the morning, but, being super optimists, we kept on trying to make ourselves believe that it was going to cease at any moment, and did not cape up. Consequently we became wetter and wetter until by this time we were soaked to the skin and then what was the use of caping up, as we should only boil. So there you are. If we had only known it was going to rain we could have left our capes at home.

Leaving the Moorcock Inn, a drop and a climb, then a long drop brought us to Hardraw Inn where we had lunch and then paid a visit to the waterfall before making a move in the direction of home. We now donned our capes and commenced the easy run through Wensleydale with its many long freewheels. We rapidly passed through Askrigg, Carperby and Redmire to Wensley. As we descended the hill down from Carperby Ken flashed by us with a cry of 'Can't stop, brakes won't act'. Round the corner he went and down to his doom. No! He had managed all the corners safely so it was a case of 'all's well that ends well'! From Wensley we continued through East Witton, Masham and West Tanfield to Ripon. We just hit Ripon at the 'right' time as the races were leaving and the town was a solid mass of buses, cars and pedestrians. However, we fought our way through to safety and covered the remaining twenty-three miles through Borough Bridge and Green Hammerton to York and at Grimston Bar had tea. Tea over, the clouds rolled away, leaving a clear sky overhead for the run home.

$$\begin{array}{ccc} \text{Mileage} & \text{Sunday} & 151 \\ & \text{Monday} & \underline{124} \\ & & 275 \end{array}$$

The Groove End Crossing – 1935

'Groove End? Never heard of it'. Thus was I greeted when I made the suggestion that we should include this crossing in our Jubilee weekend adventures. Actually Groove End is at the extreme end of Walden Dale and my idea was that we should cross from Starbottom over the Fells and down into Walden Dale and proceed down this dale to West Burton. I had had a strange weakness for this track ever since two Otley campers described to me how they had tackled it and after struggling over moor and bog for the best part of a day, had finished up with a night in the wilds – lost. I don't know why, but the thought of being utterly and absolutely lost somewhere in a wild mountainous or moorland district has always had a deep fascination for me, and here, I thought, was yet another opportunity to try my luck. Had I bothered to think further I would have realised that with a pack like the HRs for companions some chump was bound to discover our whereabouts when we appeared, to all intents and purposes, well and truly lost.

Well, with some persuasion the others agreed to the Groove End business, and when the time eventually came for the Jubilee celebrations to commence we left Hull, eleven strong, intent on getting the fullest value for money from the two days respite.

Needless to say, we left home at midnight on the Saturday. Things went very favourably during the night and in good time we were partaking of breakfast at Grassington, and later, with every prospect of a glorious day ahead, we moved off up Wharfedale as far as Starbotton.

At Starbotton, of course, things were to commence happening, and a halt was called while various articles of clothing, deemed unnecessary for the struggle before us, were stowed away in bags. By this time the temperature had risen to such an extent that one by one the party began to trickle into the local houses of refreshment with obvious intentions. While awaiting their reappearance I enquired of a dusty old farmer nearby what he considered to be the best way of reaching Groove End. With a delightful flow of local dialect he described in detail what, to his way of thinking, was the ideal method of crossing Walden Beck, and when he had departed and the rest of our party had returned from their imbibing expedition, we compared his route with the map. No, we decided, that most certainly wasn't the best way over. You see this chap had probably spent the whole of his life on the fells, and knew them like the back of his hand, so how could his knowledge be compared with our own: we, who had never explored a square inch of the district ere this. Yes, or rather, no, he was wrong. We then plotted out our route – a route, as events were to prove, which was to lead us into adventure – stark and real.

Trekking off by the back of the inn we struck off up a rough walled roadway on a savage gradient, keeping Cam Gill Beck on our left. In rather less than half a mile we had been lifted high out of the valley, and here where the road curled back on itself in its effort to find the easiest path up the severe fellside, some of us halted to see what Wharfedale looked like from this altitude. And a glorious picture we were rewarded with – every white-washed farmhouse and every tree visible in detail on its shelving green slope. The white road – a mere thread, carrying black specs backwards and forwards like ants; the holiday traffic so far below us that not a vestige of its blare and roar reached our ears. Ourselves and the curlews – sunshine – invigorating atmosphere – peace!

Soon the road, such as it was, ceased to exist, and the bare fells were ours completely – and here the party split, Eddie as usual taking two or three toughs striding ahead. We shed more of our clothing, and were now riding in the very minimum covering. The going became hard – harder than I can possibly describe – we struggled up a bank, almost perpendicular, with next to no foothold, sweating and straining, some grumbling more than a little. We were by this time nearing the end of our tether, and the stupendous effort entailed in scaling this cliff pretty nearly finished us off altogether. Scrambling out onto the open fell with the top tubes of our cycles almost severing shoulders, we staggered on over uneven ridges, frightfully weary. During all this struggle we were not sure where we were heading, merely hoping that in our line of progress lay Groove End. A succession of squelchy treacherous bogs now came along to liven things up, and when we were not stumbling wearily over the everlasting ridges, we were floundering, cursing, into the bogs, sometimes ankle deep, sometimes almost knee deep. What a weird sensation it is to stumble into a bog. You commence sinking, and fear strikes at your heart, and your stomach seemingly comes up into your throat, and your breath departs *en masse*! What with one thing and another we now felt like sinking to the ground and expiring. Then along came old man thirst. We were almost ready to commit murder for a mouthful of water, and each time we topped a ridge we staggered down the other side to the inevitable beck only to find this as dry as the proverbial bone. However, the old Hardriders' spirit was now in evidence and inner feelings were concealed.

There appeared no prospects whatever of reaching any habitation where refreshment might be obtained and we were faced with immediate extinction, when crawling over the thousandth ridge we espied a little spring bubbling delightfully from a fissure. Instantly one and all came to life and throwing ourselves on our stomachs drew in great gulps of the icy fluid.

We lingered awhile here to eat up our remaining provisions, before proceeding in the direction of Walden Head – actually passing close by Buckden Pike.

The valley opened out ahead, and away in the distance a farm house became visible. From where we stood the fells dropped steeply to meet the uncertain twists of the Walden Beck. Cautiously we commenced the descent, but tiring of this and eager to reach the floor of the valley we tried hurrying things up a bit until, missing my footing, I made the next dozen feet in one, landing on my back in a bog.

At long, long last we reached Walden Head Farm to the amazement of the inhabitants, who turned out in a body to gaze upon these poor relics of humanity. Before departing we caused many gallons of milk to disappear, afterwards giving a demonstration of such things as derailleur gears etc.

The run down to West Burton was heaven itself, a glorious narrow lane taking us at a rapid speed to our destination.

The remainder of our tour went off without anything out of the ordinary happening; one couldn't go far wrong in the existing weather, and when we reached home on the Sunday night it was with memories of a truly outstanding run.

An Evening Ride – 1930

I am seated on my office stool, gazing up at a patch of sky which shows above the high buildings opposite, when my thoughts turn to that wonderful old bike standing idly against a wall at home. For two whole days we have not been on the road and I thereupon decide that we shall have a ride over the Wolds together this evening.

5.30 p.m. comes along, the office door slams, the key turns in the lock and I stride off in the direction of my home two miles distant.

Arriving home at 5.55 p.m., I immediately demolish the tea which awaits me and fly off to change into shorts etc.

I then turn on the water in my lamp, apply a match, close the front with a snap, pull on a pair of gloves and I am ready for the off.

A glance at my watch tells me that it is 7 o'clock, so having sung out good-bye to my mother I wheel my bike out into the street and move off.

I soon reach the end of the street and turn into the main thoroughfare and pass quickly between rows of gaily lit shops, and in a few minutes leave behind the discordant clamour of trams, and pass on into the night. I have the road to myself. All is silent save for the faint hum of well inflated tyres on the dry road. The night is gloriously clear although it is November. I glance over my shoulder and see the beautiful crescent shaped moon sailing along just nicely clear of the horizon. Straight ahead of me is that arrangement of stars known, among other names, as the Plough. My bike seems to be running especially well this evening, and the road is slipping away beneath the wheels with hardly any effort on my part. I round a bend, then pass a cluster of cottages which represent the village of Dunswell. Then ahead of me a number of red lights tell me I am approaching the scene of road mending operations. These I quickly drop behind along with the rather attractive watchman's fire, which is glowing bright in the keen night air. I see by the position of the watchman's hut that what breeze there is, is blowing from a south-westerly direction. Passing through Woodmansey I catch a glimpse across the fields of the two mile distant Beverley Minster, looking very ghostly in the moonlight. A few minutes' riding brings me to the outskirts of the Minster Town. I soon pass through its twisting streets, past the Minster and then up a slight rise on to south parts of the Westwood. The road rises steadily and I press harder on the pedals and soon my whole body is glowing. My lamp lights up a notice warning me that there is a gate ahead. This turns out to be open so I ride on without having to dismount.

Another mile brings me to Walkington, and, as I pedal rapidly through the village, a group of villagers give me a 'Good night' as I pass and with an answering 'Good night' I sail onwards and commence climbing again towards the summit. A plover flies up with a screech from a field on my right on my approach. An oblong of orange light appears ahead of me and a few minutes later the dark outline of a farmhouse floats past me. I am then riding between rows of sturdy beeches and I know that I am nearing the summit. A pond reflects the moonlight into my eyes with a quick flash and then my wheels crunch through some fallen leaves. There is an occasional crack as I ride over one of the numerous beech nuts which are scattered about the road. As I pass High Hunsley House a dog barks a warning, then I reach the cross-roads. I ride straight on and another mile brings me to the sharp drop to the Market Weighton to South Cave road. I dismount and gaze about me. The cluster of lights over there on the right I tell myself will be Market Weighton. Straight ahead I pick out the lights of scattered farms, whilst on my left are the rather bright lights of South Cave Station, and there further off I see the broad silver ribbon of the moonlit River Humber. In the middle of the river a light ship is blinking in and out. Across the river is the dim outline of the Lincolnshire Wolds on which I discern more twinkling lights, and there over the horizon is the fluctuating glow thrown up by the Scunthorpe Iron Works.

After watching this flush up and die down for several minutes I turn once again to my bicycle propped up at the side of the road. I put on a scarf as the swift run downhill will be rather chilly. I get my feet into the straps and pedal joyously down the hill. Faster and faster I pedal and the wind rushes past my ears with a roar. With a bob of its white tail, a rabbit darts across my path, runs along the hedge and then, finding an opening, promptly disappears from view. I put on my brakes as I approach the main road and reaching the corner swing to the left towards South Cave. Another long drop and a short climb and I pass the station and next I am riding under the dark walls of South Cave Castle, and then pass by the gates silhouetted against the moon. I then pedal gaily down into the village, past the clock tower by which I see that the time is 8.25 p.m. and up the little hill at the far side of the village. I reach the top and glance back and down on to the moonlit roofs of the houses, above which float a few wisps of smoke.

My feet begin to feel rather numb and I pedal faster and pump the warm blood down into my toes. I am feeling intensely fit and my bike leaps forwards in answer to the increased pressure on the pedals. As I pass a clump of trees the moon twinkles in and out among the trunks and then my lamp lights up a signpost – Hull to the left – Brough straight on. I swing round to the left and soon leave Elloughton behind. I turn on the water regulator of my lamp a notch as the moon is now slipping over the horizon and the road is darker. A rustle of leaves as I pass a tree tells me that a breeze is springing up. I glide through Welton and, glancing to the right, I see a train worming its way along by the river, its engine sending out cascades of sparks. I pass through Melton and am soon dropping down into Ferriby, over the cross-roads and on towards Hessle. Pedalling blithely over the undulations, I turn to the left at Hesslewood cross-roads and a few minutes later turn into a new road which cuts out Hessle. As I turn into this road the lights of Hull are spread out before me, and the thought strikes me that from here at any rate Hull is beautiful. The road has not been officially opened and I have repeatedly to dodge heaps of gravel. Then after crawling under a barrier I ride on towards the first street lamp. Passing cautiously through the conglomeration of trams and buses, I eventually arrive back at my garden gate. I pass through the gate, slide the bolt into place, put back my bike in the place I had taken it from and go forth in search of supper, my heart singing within me.

Appendix
The Principal Moutain Passes
Ascended

1.	BAVELLA (Cor)	1,243m	4,078ft.
2.	BRENNER (It)	1,362m	4,468ft.
3.	CAMPO LUNGO (It)	1,891m	6,404ft.
4.	COSTA LUNGA (It)	1,783m	5,580ft.
5.	FALZAREGO (It)	2,105m	6,950ft.
6.	FUELA (Sw)	2,388m	7,835ft.
7.	FURKA (Sw)	2,431m	7,980ft.
8.	GALIBIER (Fr)	2,556m	8,386ft.
9.	GARDENA (It)	2,021m	6,956ft.
10.	GEMMI (Sw)	2,329m	7,941ft.
11.	GRIESSEN (Au)	968m	3,176ft.
12.	GRIMSELL (Sw)	2,164m	7,098ft.
13.	GR.GLOCKNER (Au)	2,572m	8,438ft.
14.	HARDANGER (Nor)	1,381m	4,531ft.
15.	HEMSEDAL (Nor)	1,137m	3,630ft.
16.	ISELBERG (Au)	1,204m	3,950ft.
17.	ISERAN (Fr)	2,769m	9,085ft.
18.	KESSELBERG (Bav)	914m	3,000ft.
19.	KNIE (Aus)	914m	3,000ft.
20.	LAUTERET (Fr)	2,058m	6,752ft.
21.	DES.MOSSES (Sw)	1,449m	4,750ft.
22.	MT. CENIS (Fr)	2,083m	6,834ft.
23.	MT.GENEVRE (Fr)	1,894m	5,919ft.
24.	OFEN (Sw)	2,155m	7,068ft.
25.	OBERALP (SW)	2,046m	6,710ft.
26.	SAANAN MOSER (Sw)	1,284m	4,210ft.
27.	ST. ANGELO (It)	1,755m	5,758ft.
28.	ST. BERNARD (G) (Fr)	2,467m	8,092ft.
29.	ST. BERNARD (L) (Fr)	2,188m	7,178ft
30.	ST. WOLFGANGS (Sw)	1,635m	5,363ft
31.	SCHARNITZ (Bav)	958m	3,133ft

32.	SELJESTAD (Nor)	1,065m	3,494ft.
33.	SELLA (It)	2,237m	7,339ft.
34.	SORBA (Cor)	1,305m	4,281ft.
35.	SPLUGEN (Sw)	2,119m	6,944ft.
36.	STEIN (Au)	1,036m	3,400ft.
37.	STELVIO (It)	2,767m	9,045ft.
38.	STRUB (Au)	697m	2,287ft.
39.	TELEGRAPH (Fr)	1,530m	5,020ft.
40.	TRE CROCI (It)	1,808m	5,936ft.
41.	VAACHIA (Cor)	1,188m	3,898ft.
42.	VALDRES (Nor)	1,073m	3,520ft.
43.	VERDE (Cor)	1,187m	3,896ft.
44.	VERGIO (Cor)	1,464m	4,803ft.

Austria (Au)   Bavaria (Bav)   Corsica (Cor)
France (Fr)   Italy (It)   Norway (Nor)
Switzerland   (Sw)